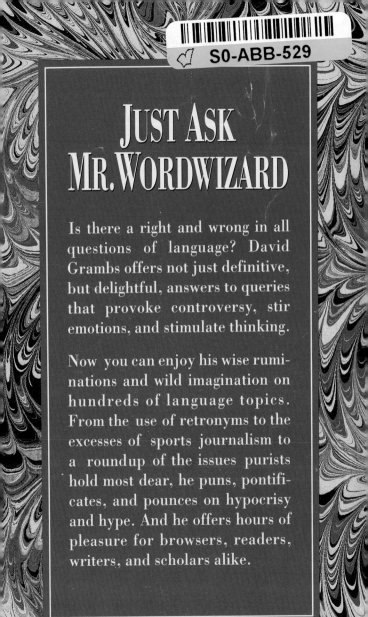

JUST ASK
MR. WORDWIZARD

Is there a right and wrong in all questions of language? David Grambs offers not just definitive, but delightful, answers to queries that provoke controversy, stir emotions, and stimulate thinking.

Now you can enjoy his wise ruminations and wild imagination on hundreds of language topics. From the use of retronyms to the excesses of sports journalism to a roundup of the issues purists hold most dear, he puns, pontificates, and pounces on hypocrisy and hype. And he offers hours of pleasure for browsers, readers, writers, and scholars alike.

HOW WORDY ARE YOU?

What's the longer word that each of these shortened
forms came from?
BRIG, MOB, PROPS, CAB, PANTS,
SYNC, PERK, FLIP

(answers: brigantine, *mobile vulgus*, properties, cabriolet,
pantaloons, synchronization,
perquisite, flippant)

Who contributed these words or phrases to English?
PANDEMONIUM
LUNATIC FRINGE
ANESTHESIA
BLACKMAIL
SELF-HELP

(answers: John Milton, Teddy Roosevelt, Oliver Wendell
Holmes, Sir Walter Scott, Thomas Carlyle)

Which lost positives (the words after the parentheses)
were genuine words at one time?
(un)couth
(in)scrutable
(dis)traught
(de)molition
(un)kempt

(answers: couth, scrutable, molition, kempt)

Want to know more? Let a master wordsmith entertain,
educate, and enlighten you in—
Just Ask Mr. Wordwizard

JUST ASK MR. WORDWIZARD

*"Sentences Repaired,
Words Offered,
Ignorance Thwarted"*

David Grambs

LAUREL

To Bea and Bunny

An Intrepid Linguist Book

Published by
Dell Publishing
a division of
Bantam Doubleday Dell Publishing Group, Inc.
1540 Broadway
New York, New York 10036

The trademark THE INTREPID LINGUIST LIBRARY and its related "ILL" logo are registered in the U.S. Patent and Trademark Office.

The trademarks Laurel® and Dell® are registered in the U.S. Patent and Trademark Office.

ISBN: 0-440-21719-9

Printed in the United States of America

Published simultaneously in Canada

February 1995

10 9 8 7 6 5 4 3 2 1

OPM

Contents

JUST ASK MR. WORDWIZARD

DISAGREEING TO DISAGREE

WORD OF THE WEEK: *idiolect*—an individual's unique language

QUOTE OF THE WEEK: "Words are, of course, the most powerful drug used by mankind."

—RUDYARD KIPLING

Is there a right and wrong in all questions of language?

"Hopefully your weekly language column for *The Woofton Wind Sock* will be more unique and different than others and will impact the whole gauntlet of language issues for we whom aren't disinterested," reads one of my first letters, from Ms. D.N. "We need somebody here in Woofton to flaunt the illiterates who don't care."

Letters from Woofton language-lovers and -watchers are already coming in.

It's a little discouraging to receive a well-wishing letter that begins with *hopefully* and contains seven other infelicities (an infelicity, language-lovers, is a verbal ugliness), particularly when it's from one of our local high school English teachers. But I refuse to be discouraged.

So here I am, dedicated to being your phantom words-and-stuff columnist, your linguistic general practitioner, complete with a shingle hung out.

Readers of the *Wind Sock* all know about the recent

state literacy study that came down a little hard (no, it's not *hardly*) on our fine town of Woofton. The Department of State Education has designated us one of seven Grammatical Disaster Areas in our fair state. Woofton a "community of beetling lowbrows and rhinestones in the rough"? Of "television- and video-addicted troglodytes"? A "depressing whistle-stop for any train of thought"?

We Wooftonians know better. (Our publisher at *The Woofton Wind Sock,* Mr. Carwell, is allowing considerable space for this column.)

Rest assured, I'm not a self-appointed guardian of correctness. I hope I'm not a self-annointed one, either. Like anybody who cares about the cause of good English, I have my own barking kennel of loud pet peeves. But I'd rather think of this column as a causerie. A causerie is not, as a newspaper colleague of mine thought, a French bridge over troubled waters. A causerie is an informal chat or article. We hope you'll join the chat hereabouts each week.

But what *is* right—or *who* is right—when it comes to questions of proper English usage?

"Mr. Wordwizard" is the correct answer—but only in this column, and maybe not even then. If English were a simpler tongue, the question of who the real authority is wouldn't forever be such a knotty issue.

Take any knotty verbal issue. How many viewpoints can there be regarding what is correct or preferable?

More than you might think. For example, one of the pioneering features of the *American Heritage Dictionary* (1969) was to capsulize the verdicts of a so-called Usage Panel regarding typical questions of usage, from the importance of a distinction between *disinterested* and *uninterested* to the allowability of the introductory *hopefully.* The panel was composed of more than a hundred presumed experts, most of them editors, authors, teachers, essayists, or journalists. Panelists were called upon to express their views on hundreds of usage issues being touched on in the dictionary.

Out of all of these, the American Heritage Usage Panelists were unanimous in their yes-or-no opinion in only *one* case: disapproval of using the word *simultaneous* as an adverb. For the record, the panel came closest (more than 90 percent of the members agreeing) to unanimity in disapproving *ain't I* and *between you and I* in writing; *thusly;* the dialectal expression *but what; debut* as a verb; the plural *medias; their own* after a singular antecedent; *myself (instead of me)* in a compound object; *type* for *type of;* and qualifying the word *unique* with *rather* or *most.* In voting yes, the panel came closest (more than 90 percent) to unanimity in approving the use of *dropout* as a noun and of *slow* as an adverb.

That leaves a lot of disagreement among them regarding almost eight hundred other language issues.

Over the years there have been numerous purported usage authorities or experts. Many have or have had strong opinions, but in arguing their case about this or that (or about *this* versus *that),* too often they have not told the whole story regarding the historical evidence or the pros and cons of an issue. As *Webster's Dictionary of English Usage* points out, "many pedagogues seem reluctant to share the often complicated facts about English with their students." To "students" can be added "readers."

To illustrate this, take the classic issue of *flaunt* versus *flout,* as exemplified in the letter-writer's line that opened this column: "We need somebody here in Woofton to flaunt the illiterates who don't care."

Literate people know that whereas *flaunt* means "to display or make known in a showy way," *flout,* quite a different kettle of fish, means "to show contemptuous disregard for, to scorn." Yet as our Woofton English teacher demonstrates, people are forever confusing the meanings of the two words, usually using *flaunt* where *flout* is what is meant. In derivation or etymology *flaunt* comes from a Scandinavian word meaning "to rush around," *flout* from a Middle English word for "flute."

The distinction here—which is "right"—should be as

cut and dried as a posy of desert flowers. But suppose
more people are using *flaunt* incorrectly than are using
it correctly? Suppose one dictionary now lists *flaunt* as a
synonym for *flout*? Suppose, hypothetically, a host of
usage experts conveniently convene in Woofton to settle
matters. Surely, when asked "Is it permissible to use the
word *flaunt* for what has been traditionally expressed by
flout?" they'll all agree it's not permissible?

Surely not.

And all for different reasons, from A to Z.

Expert A says no, it's not permissible to use *flaunt* to
mean *flout,* because it's plain wrong, a misuse of the
word, a gaucherie.

Expert B says yes, it's all right, because the majority
of people now so use it; it's well established, a lost battle.

Expert C says no, it violates the original sense of
flaunt etymologically.

Expert D says yes, it seems logical or natural enough
a development linguistically because of the similarity of
sound.

Expert E says no, it's just faddish, an unfortunate current trend to be resisted. We have to think long-term,
historically. As Jacques Barzun says, Shouldn't we look
ahead?

Expert F says yes, it's okay, but only in informal or
colloquial contexts.

Expert G says no, because this use is fostered by the
brainless media or by politicians and jargon-users, and
they don't deserve to win.

Expert H says yes, because it's a finicky or petty matter, and to be fussy about it is to be pedantic or affected.

Expert I says no, the distinction between the two
words is definitely worth keeping and defending.

Expert J says yes, but it's allowable only in speech, not
in writing.

Expert K says no, the misuse may be spreading, but
that's only because American education and literacy are
currently in a pretty sorry state.

Expert L says yes, as dictionary X says that *flaunt* may be used to mean *flout*.

Expert M says no, as dictionary Y says that it may not be so used.

Expert N says yes, as three dictionaries say it's okay while only two say it's wrong.

Expert O says no, because educated people would never make such a mistake.

Expert P says yes, because it's elitist or Eurocentric to insist on the distinction in meaning. It's a threat to multiculturalism.

Expert Q says no, because it's frowned upon by usage guide X, the best of all usage books.

Expert R says yes, because, really, any listener will usually know what the speaker means. The context always makes it quite clear.

And so forth. So forth, because if the case in point involved two other words or a controversial trendy phrase, still other rationales could be offered: that the expression in question is awkward or stilted, that it's an established idiom and by now set in stone, or that it's historically justifiable because the expression used to mean . . .

Please consider this a little inaugural object lesson, a reminder that reputable language authorities often flauntingly disagree about what one may properly and allowably flout. So many people wish there would always be nice and tidy right answers to language questions. It's very frustrating that there are not. We all *want* to be one united people when it comes to language issues, don't we? We want English to have clear rights and wrongs. In this sense, you can say we disagree to disagree.

Mr. Wordwizard's opinion is that the well-wishing Ms. D.N. ought not to have flaunted her flouting of good usage and that *flaunt* should not be used for *flout*.

Meanwhile, I hope you will find this weekly column pleasantly instructive or diverting and do your part to advance literacy in Woofton by purchasing a good dictionary and spending some time with it throughout the week. Something to think about: Language is liquid, not solid or, let us hope, gaseous. But if you don't use your dictionary, the language surrounding you will use you.

Is there a word you can't think of or a rare word you'd like to know about? Drop me a line.

Have you noticed a spelling mistake in this column? You should have—but not more than one, I hope. In each Wordwizard column will be implanted one deliberate misspelling. The first three callers phoning *The Woofton Wind Sock* and correctly identifying the error will receive a free college dictionary.

Nominal Falsies

WORD OF THE WEEK: *stigmeology*—the art of punctuation

QUOTE OF THE WEEK: "Who does not know another language, does not know his own."

—JOHANN WOLFGANG VON GOETHE

You see them in the newspaper every day and hardly notice them. They're nominal falsies.

"I don't like being labeled" is something just about all of us have said at one time or another. But as if some friend had stuck a tag on your back for laughs, you have only to become newsworthy—and not even in a criminal way—to have a good chance of getting stuck with a label.

Welcome to a look at what journalists and language-watchers call variously false titles, bogus titles, or coined titles—or nominal falsies.

It would seem that categorizing people doesn't get very far these oversensitive days. American society is no longer merely litigious. It's label-sensitive. Traditionally libel and slander have never been sanctioned, meaning that you can't call somebody a politically corrupt, leprous murderer with impunity. More recently, certain epithets, labels, or even associations have become instantly unwelcome to women or members of minority groups. Even pronouns have become sensitive issues, and prop-

erly so: Any instance of sexist writing is swiftly un-
manned of presumptuously masculine pronouns—that
generic *he*—or patriarchal vocabulary.

We deplore obvious stereotypes and name-calling.
Yet most of us don't bat an eye at more subtle labeling
in print. For instance, "recently imprisoned former congressman Smith." Or is it "Recently Imprisoned Former
Congressman Smith," capitalizing the whole schmear?
In writing it's legitimate to "title" somebody descrip-
tively in a few words, isn't it? To avoid a separate sentence and to save space?

About traditional honorifics and professional titles—
Professor, Assemblywoman, Doctor—there has never
been any question. But when it comes to other vocations
or livelihoods, labeling people can get tricky, particularly when several descriptives are piled up. What about
"art dealer John Doe"—or "discount art dealer John
Doe"? "Typist John Doe"—or "part-time typist John
Doe"? "Distinguished poet Jane Doe"—or "distinguished local poet Jane Doe"? Is it right for a writer to
single out one aspect of a person's life and make that a
label when introducing that person in print?

Once mostly a noted mannerism of *Time* magazine,
questionable made-up titles are now virtually de rigeur
in journalism. (*Time* was also famous for its lead-off
verbs, a style classically satirized by Wolcott Gibb's line
"Backward ran sentences until reeled the mind." Excuse
me—that's "writer and critic Wolcott Gibbs.") They are
called false or bogus titles because they are conferred
only in the newsroom or writer's study.

The false title, writes usage authority (not a false title) Roy Copperud, "is never heard in speech, which
often is a good model for clarity in writing."

But false titles are often criticized also because they
are easily avoidable, with an appositive construction. Instead of saying "lawyer and rock drummer John Doe,"
one can avoid the glib up-front characterization by writing "John Doe, a lawyer who is also a rock drummer."
By resorting to the false title, the writer does not show

the power of appositive thinking. The nominal falsie saves a few words and jazzes up the copy a bit. (It also sometimes spares the writer from deciding whether somebody is, say, "noted tenor," "a noted tenor," or "the noted tenor," where the mere choice of article colors how renowned somebody is supposed to be.)

From our national newsmagazines and supermarket tabloids to television ("We'll be right back with doubles tennis star . . ."), pigeonholing titles are everywhere. Who notices them? Or that they can be quite arbitrary or too facile—and are often used primarily to affect a breezy, all-knowing style?

When the descriptives really get piled up (or on)— "foreign-educated aeronautical computer systems analyst John Doe"—it can be hard on the reader, and maybe a little ridiculous. We get chains of stickers— concatenated characterizations. We get what's called *morkrumbo,* an old term for a kind of routine journalistic writing and in particular for bogus titling.

Clearly, using false titles is a slippery slope. It can lead beyond dubious vocational and avocational characterizations to more judgmental adjectives. If "distinguished" can be used to label somebody, how about "undistinguished"? If "longtime Hollywood mogul and celebrated romancer . . . ," how about "would-be Hollywood mogul and former ladies' man . . ."?

The message for you here is to be more aware that the identifying tags you read or hear every day are worth being less unconscious about. They can be debatable—maybe you're being swayed or misinformed in a subtle way (to say nothing of the victimized descriptee).

But the slippery slope of false titles opens entertaining possibilities, and why should we spare ourselves from contributing a few of our own making? Why not a little frivolous verbal Pin the Tail on the Donkey?

What if one had to cover a posh society party for the society page of the newspaper?

"The guests of honor at Tuesday evening's charity bash at the Laroque Pavilion were ambivalent feminist

Wendy Solomon and distracted neurosurgeon Peter Bourse, but the real star of this fabulous soiree was indenial reprobate Silvester DeLeon. Seen awhirl on the dance floor—to the strains of the band of flamboyant heterosexual Ted Kittington—were hair-plugged labor mediator Sam Flask with perfume-drenched overdresser Barbara Nell, token jogger Jim Dalrymple with empowered-tripping job hopper Maureen Sayreson, breast-fixated and halitosis-recovering widow-wooer D. Fred Armis with world-class party flirt Tootsie Carbone, and between-jobs and unemployable vocational consultant Miller Yates with careful-pronouncing nitpicker Phoebe Erlangen. Introductions to both Miss Solomon and Dr. Bourse, who addressed the attendees, were made by unfulfilled plutocrat Dennis Gobb. Also seen moving suavely about the pavilion's gilded-stucco rooms and terraces were superannuated party-crasher Bob Sinton, compulsive reiterater and paraphraser Alice Jermay, recovering codependent Brenda Southers, conveniently hearing-impaired money-launderer Carlos Manila, acquitted drugstore shoplifter C. N. Chelfield II, and philanthropist and ingenius malingerer Carlton Woods."

I forgot to mention that false titles can be a lot of fun, too.

The deliberately misspelled word in last week's column was _self-annointed_. It's _self-anointed_.

RETRONYMS

Synonyms, antonyms. How about retronyms?

The word *retro*, you may have noticed in your magazine reading, has become popular lately.

The meaning of the prefix *retro-* is "back" or "backward," but the use of this trendy word element seems to be going forward everywhere. Back in the astronautic 1960s we heard it mostly as attached to *rocket* (the firing of), but nowadays the hyphen seems to have been kicked away to make *retro* a word by itself, signifying that somebody or something is an old or formerly seen or onetime specimen. An architectural style is retro. An outfit that somebody wears to a downtown city club is retro. An individual's social or political views are considered retro.

So that to be retro is to be a throwback. Or maybe something or somebody worth throwing back—the word is often used with a bit of smugness or condescension, an implication that the what or who that is retro is not quite up to date, is not hip or with it. (When it comes to trendy expressions, maybe it's just as good to be against-it as with-it.)

Two words related in meaning are *atavistic* and *recrudescent.* Something atavistic is something that recurs or shows up again in a later generation, usually a trait in an organism. Something recrudescent is something that revives or becomes active again, or rather that breaks out again—it's usually something undesirable, such as a disease or an unfortunate social trend. But these are big words. *Retro* is nicely new-fashioned to mean old-fashioned. (It comes not from *retrograde* but from the French word *retrospectif.*)

Which brings us to the fact that words or phrases can be retro as well.

For example, there used to be just guitars. Then they were seemingly superceded by electric guitars, and far too many of them. There were so many that guitars were now assumed to be electric ones, making it necessary to find a way to refer to the old nonelectric kind. Thus was born *acoustic guitar.* (An old and rare word for the original of a name is *protonym.*)

Such a remodified, compensatory term we now call a retronym, for which we can thank ultimate language columnist William Safire; he tells us that it was coined by writer Frank Mankiewicz. Unlike synonyms or antonyms or homonyms, retronyms become expedient when progress or technology or mere changing times newfangles something, necessitating an added explanatory word to denote the old variety.

Other retronyms we use today include *silent movie* (versus *talkie), natural grass* (versus *artificial), analog watch* (versus *digital), pocket watch* (versus *wrist), hardcover book* (versus *paperback), prop plane* (versus *jet), steam locomotive* (versus *diesel), free weights* (versus *exercise machine), inpatient* (versus *outpatient), raw sewage* (versus *treated), rotary telephone* (versus *touchtone),* and *stage play* (versus *television).* Similarly, contemporary developments often necessitate using a *non-* or *un-* or *pre-* prefix to be clear about older or now less common varieties, such as a *nonfilter cigarette,* an *unborn child,* or *pre-cable television.*

The retronym, then, is a semantic restorative, an old-fashioner. It's like a maiden name that needs mentioning.

Moving right along seems to be the way of the world, and of language. More and more words don't mean quite what they used to. But we'll always have occasion to refer to previous incarnations of things or beings, and linguistically (and creatively) we will have to keep taking designative steps backward. Retronyms are bound to keep on coming.

And Mr. Wordwizard thinks a few in particular may be long overdue. Won't you contribute by sending in those you'd suggest?

Here are a few I'd suggest:

double-parent household. In our age of domestic disintegration, we hear the phrase *single-parent household* so often that the old-fashioned normal home situation begs for a new term. Will double-parent households be recognized minority groups within ten years?

participatory sex. Erotic activity between the sexes used to be pretty straightforward. Now all we hear about is *phone sex,* or touchtone autoeroticism. When we don't hear about that, we hear about *safe sex.* A retronym is needed to remind us that in normal societies it just took two, without insulation, to tango.

pretycoon athlete. A pre-1980s professional athlete who is not obscenely oversalaried and underexerting, before the age of millionaire mediocrities.

uncategorical American. A pre-1970s American, not self-identifying with a factional minority or ethnic "community." A melting-pot nonhyphenate.

pedantic pop. Popular music lyrics that were clearly articulated and understandable.

naked poster. Any advertising placard not covered with graffiti.

bare-eared exerciser. A jogger, biker, or health club member who can work out without wearing a headset.

<u>*warm cash*</u> (or *over-the-counter cash).* Money received from a human bank teller.

<u>*promiscuous food.*</u> Food enjoyed without dieting obsession or guilt.

<u>*she-free English.*</u> English before the worry and sensitivity about generic male pronouns' being sexist.

<u>*penile pregnancy.*</u> Old-fashioned insemination involving no surrogate mother, artificial insemination, or in vitro fertilization.

unacted news. Local television newscasting before it became a performance of first names and false bonhomie by a news "team."

<u>*wordy history.*</u> World or American history learned from books, before it was learned through television movies, visual aids, and theme parks.

<u>*sensuous Colgate.*</u> A metal toothpaste tube, back in the days when you could have the fun of rolling them up.

I'll have more to say about some other *-nyms* in a future column.

The deliberately misspelled word in last week's column was <u>*de rigeur.*</u> It's <u>*de rigueur.*</u>

CHAMELEON SYNONYMS

Words, some people think, never bear repeating.

"The store has nice enough merchandise," goes one recent letter to this column, "but when I went to the shop recently, I noticed several misspellings on signs around the boutique. This is an emporium I'm not sure I'll go back to."

Similarly, another letter, from a local professor, reads, "I try to be patient with students, but not all pupils deserve patience, I'm afraid, particularly when comparing these instructees with other undergraduates."

Similarly? Maybe the operative word here should be *dissimilarly* or *variously,* in that both of the above examples brandish needless synonyms: *store, shop, boutique, emporium;* and *students, pupils, instructees, undergraduates.* Variety may be the spice of life, but it isn't always the spice of writing, not when it is needless, strained, or confusing to the reader. The first writer above, in order not to repeat the word *store,* follows it with *shop, bou-*

tique, and *emporium,* a little synonym dance complete with castanettes.

Why? Doubtless out of the common notion that one should never repeat a nonminor word within the same sentence, or within the space of twenty (or some other arbitrary number) words or X number of lines.

It's fine to vary one's wording and keep the writing lively and interesting, but not to the point where it is a noticeable mannerism, almost the symptom of a phobia.

Possibly you're a secret synonymy quick-change artist yourself. You don't want to be monotonous in your writing. Now hear this: Analyze monotonous prose, and you'll find that the cause is *not* really the repeating of the key words. It's the repeating of key words without saying anything new, sentence after sentence. It's the uninspired phrasing (syntax), general wordiness, and triteness of thought behind the writing.

Monotonous repetition can often be avoided merely by using pronouns, by a little rephrasing, or by ellipsis— that is, omitting the particular word the second time around (compounding), or using one clause instead of two.

The idea that a word—usually a noun or verb—ought never be repeated "close by" is a false one. The term for such stylistic avoidance behavior is, courtesy of the great H. W. Fowler (to be a subject of a future column) in his classic *Modern English Usage,* elegant variation.

He did not intend it as a term of praise. If anything, elegant variation (or conspicuous variation, as usage authority Roy Copperud calls it) is the giveaway of the second-rate writer. Among its most consistent (or is it varying?) perpetrators today are sportswriters and sports-speakers. Turn on your local news, and you'll invariably (or variably) learn that whereas the Twins merely defeated the Red Sox, the Orioles edged the A's, the White Sox trounced the Rangers, the Mariners outlasted the Yankees, and the Royals put away the Tigers. Of course, there can be a difference between an edging and a trouncing, but usually the verbs here are varied solely for variety's sake. Elegant variation can be an ill-advised attempt to "keep ahead of" the reader.

Another form this synonym-mania takes is the altering of so-called dialogue verbs in fiction. Here, in a patch of back-and-forth dialogue, one character "says," another "rejoins" or "snaps back," a third character "notes," and a fourth "allows" before the first speaker "offers" and the third "adds." Much commercial fiction thrives on this sort of thing, but it's also a trait of otherwise good writers who should know better.

So *elegant variation* is a term you should know. It's far less familiar to people than, say, *dangling participle* or *split infinitive,* but it's worth making a part of your vocabulary because the practice is so widespread as a writing fault—even you can easily become prone to it.

Certainly, varied wording and phrasing can be a virtue in writing. But an unshakable taboo against merely repeating a word proximately is another matter indeed and has no basis. Many of literature's greatest writers have a simple style and simple diction (in the sense of vocabulary). They write in brief sentences and repeat words, often to great effect. (The deliberate repetition of words or phrases at the beginning of successive clauses or sentences is the rhetorical device of anaphora.) How many people find Hemingway's writing boring?

As British novelist and critic David Lodge points out, writing well in a style that repeats words "looks easy, but of course it isn't. The words are simple but their arrangement is not." When the right words are used again and again in a thoughtful resonant way, the effect can be hypnotic and profound, like an incantation. Lodge analyzes one paragraph in a Hemingway novel: "The incantatory rhythms and repetitions persist in the second paragraph. It would have been easy to find elegant alternatives for 'hospital,' or simply to have used the pronoun 'it' occasionally; but the hospital is the centre of the soldiers' lives, their daily place of pilgrimage, the repository of their hopes and fears, and the repetition of the word is therefore expressive."

The truth is that when writing is effective and absorbing, the reader scarcely notices repeated use of the same word.

Elegant variation, then, is the tic of the amateurish writer trying to be clever before he or she has settled into being clear and competent in style. To read a passage in which the writer conspicuously avoids using the same word twice can be like suffering through a one-man band playing a back-and-forth on different instruments, when a clearly sustained melody on one of them would be preferable.

It's a bad habit because it usually draws attention to itself or to the writer rather than to the writing. It can confuse a reader, who can only wonder why this verbal sleight-of-hand is being used. Does the writer mean a slight shift in meaning in each case? Or is there a different reason?

Usually, too, not all the synonymous expressions "work." Synonyms are not always interchangeable. Their meanings may not be exactly (enough) the same. Their connotations, overtones, and associations may not accord. Different words can be at different levels of diction, as when one of them is formal, another is archaic, and another is downright slangy. For example, a writer who is determined to keep ringing the changes may use *women* once, may follow it with *females*—and then, trapped in this game, have to resort to such an ill-advised locution as *the fair sex* or *the distaff side*. Which is to say that, one, seemingly apposite terms can not only be dubious in the same company but their supply can run out; and second, the writer who embarks on the mad dance of elegant variation usually exposes his or her limitations. The reader quickly sees that the elegant-varier is trying to be "colorful" but actually has a tin ear when it comes to nuances of word meaning.

The moral here is that one word repeated naturally or intelligently is better than four used to underestimate the reader's attention span. A flashy but rote juggling of synonyms doth not a good phrasing or prose style make. Eschew chameleon synonyms. Be colorful in your wording if you wish, but in a way that doesn't announce that you're trying too hard to be so.

The deliberately misspelled word in last week's column was *superceded*. It's *superseded*.

FRENCH FRÉS

In English nothing gives your self-confidence a little pickup quite like a little French does. And to demonstrate that this column can be not only corrective in spirit but constructive, I'm going to introduce you this week to what I call French frés (as in *phrase*). I'm taking pseudo-French liberties, as there's no such word as *fré*.

We of Woofton could use a little vocabulary spice, I think. Letters to this column show that many of you are upset about that state literacy report that described us as "ill-bred, ill-read, and don't know what's ill-said." Our local junior college, Boeotia State, may have been described as "a halfway house for intellectual fetuses" and as "Operation Head Stop," but I fully expect letters will come to me from Boeotia State students that will prove otherwise.

French frés, anybody?

Although France today is less than welcoming to the infusion of English words and resultant "Franglais," we appreciative and generous Americans don't feel the same way about accepting French words into our language.

From Latin we get much of our technical and scholarly vocabulary (and words of several syllables). From German we get not only many words but our ease in joining elements to make words, technically known as agglutination. Most of our simplest words come from our forebear, Anglo-Saxon or Old English. But it was French, through the Norman invasion in 1066, that radically altered and enriched the vocabulary of English. We've continued to borrow from it, from *à la carte* to *vis-à-vis*. Our chowder is really made from the French word *chaudière*. When we sashay, we've borrowed from the French word *chasser*. When we get engaged, we might speak of our intended, but we're much more likely to speak of our fiancé or fiancée.

Those smart and intense little vowels, Gallicisms, and French-born English words give our sentences a little music, some little bells and whistles to make people sit up and take notice. (They'll notice even more when you get the French wrong: How many Americans today pronounce the final word of *coup de grace* as "grah" rather than the correct "grahs," thereby saying "blow of the meaty fat," *gras?*) Whether it's for the wrong reasons or not, whether it's all superficial or only vocabulary-deep, the sound or hint of French has cachet, a touch of class. If we put a sachet (not to be confused with sashay) in our bureau drawers, why not a little cachet in our English? Some savoir-faire, some panache?

Even when we're not measuring up, we'd rather be labeled with a word of French origin. Why make a blunder when you can make a gaffe? Why be vulgar when you can be gauche? Why be racy or dirty when you can be risqué? Why be a plebian slut who gets around when you can be a demimondaine?

For starters, you can learn ten indispensable French fré words right here.

A French fré is an adjective, found in all reputable dictionaries of English, that is useful as a descriptive of people and that ends in an *é*, or an *e* with the French acute accent. If you're not already familiar with them, these ten French frés will add a little "accent" to your observations of others.

The ten are *distingué, soigné, outré, borné, dégagé, blasé, démodé, passé, déclassé,* and *manqué.*

A *distingué* individual is one with a distinctively distinguished air, while one who is *soigné* is elegantly turned out or well-groomed. What about the person who in behavior, point of view, or lifestyle is quite bizarre or outrageous? He or she is way out, or *outré.* The individual who, more seriously, is limited or hidebound in outlook or is plain narrow-minded is *borné.* Better to be easygoing or carefree, or *dégagé.*

Of course, if you're *dégagé* for too long a time, you're in danger of becoming *blasé,* or contentedly bored or unimpressed. When somebody (or something) who has been in fashion, even a very *distingué* person, falls out of fashion, he or she is regrettably *démodé* or—with the accent more on being out-of-date—*passé.* One who has fallen not out of fashion but in social status is *déclassé.*

Finally, what of the person who has aspired and strived but never really made it except to mediocrity, the unsuccessful would-be? He or she is a writer, statesman, or playboy *manqué;* the *manqué* follows the other word, like a degree in unfulfillment.

Mr. Wordwizard guarantees that if you learn these ten handy French frés and use them intelligently and as casually as possible, you will impress other people. The light touch is all. If you're not a Francophone, or speaker of French, you certainly don't want to come across as a Francophony. Please avoid French frés if you don't wish to impress other people. Some may be so impressed that they will be afraid to ask you what your French fré word means.

If you get used to using these Gallicisms in the right way, with some unmitigated Gaul, it's bound to improve the rest of your English.

Remember to add an extra *e* to the above spellings for females.

The deliberately misspelled word in last week's column was *castanettes*. It's *castanets*.

IN DENIAL POLITICALLY

WORD OF THE WEEK: *longueur*—a dull passage in a book

QUOTE OF THE WEEK: "There is only one way to degrade mankind permanently and that is to destroy language."

—NORTHROP FRYE

Is there such a thing as damage-control English?

The danger of ignoring the formulary language of politics has never been better illustrated than by the sadly abrupt resignation of our local Woofton assemblyman Peter Swatchman. Assemblyman Swatchman, accused of shoplifting at a women's shoe store while already under indictment for embezzlement and bribery, denied all charges in resigning.

But his speech at the Woofton City Hall press conference was singularly straightforward and brief:

"It's with great regret that I have to inform you of my resignation as assemblyman, ending almost thirteen years of selfless service to the people of Woofton. Numerous accusations have been made regarding me. Although they are probably untrue, I feel at this point in time it would be better for the interests of Woofton if I were to step down. I have nothing more to say."

Whether Peter Swatchman is innocent or guilty, this plain statement may have been his greatest error. (He does deserve some credit, however, for getting in the

Watergateism *at this point in time,* by now expected of all politicians.) Why? Because in his bowing-out speech, Assemblyman Swatchman did not use the phraseology of self-righteous denial, an idiom that must be mastered by any American public servant. Instead of playing a violincello, he played a mere ukulele.

Specifically, he didn't avail himself of any of the (1) Five Dignified Conjunctions, (2) Twelve Emphatic Adverbs, and above all, (3) Twenty Oil-of-Sanctity Phrases.

This column is offered as a public service to any young Wooftonians who are considering a career, which may include a rise and a fall, in politics.

Standard political language consists not only of patriotic rhetoric (or so-called spread-eagle oratory), rhyming or alliterative slogans, gladhanding greetings, ringing but empty promises, and eloquent mudslinging. There are also times of crisis. When an officeholder is in hot water, he or she has to know how to make the right splashes verbally.

The deeds that get a politician into trouble are expressed in another kind of language, and—lucky us Americans—we get to read about it in the newspapers every other day: *peculation* or *embezzlement* (fraudulent appropriation of money), *defalcation* (misappropriation of money), *subornation* (bribing someone to break the law or "inducing" false testimony), *bilking* (cheating or defrauding), and *mulcting* (swindling or extorting). The latter word should not be confused with mulching.

All in all, any of these misdoings constitutes *malfeasance* (wrongdoing in a position of public trust) or, in that more resonant term, *graft.* We all know that many politicians like to misdo, and when it comes out that somebody's hand has been in the till, all the posse can do is (to borrow a phrase from the Watergate thriller *All the President's Men*) follow the money. Other on-the-job hobbies of public servants besides bribery and theft include arm-twisting illegal campaign contributions, cheating on taxes, and putting goldbrick or no-show relatives on the payroll *(nepotism).* Metaphorically, it's all called *greasing the palm,* and the politician who is ambitiously venal (he or she is called a *boodler*) knows that the squeaky palm gets the grease. His or her palm is often the squeaky one.

But the rhetoric of self-rightous denial is our subject: the words and phrases necessary to lend an air of dignity to any political speech denying allegations. (When a politician becomes fond of saying *Let me just say* . . . , you know he's comfortably put the truth behind him once and for all.)

Many accused officeholders resign at the very same time they deny the allegation, which is an interesting combination. But innocent or guilty, they should know that the public fully expects to hear at least a token sampling of the Five Dignified Conjunctions, the Twelve Emphatic Adverbs, and the Twenty Oil-of-Sanctity Phrases. (There is no partridge in a pear tree here.) They are face-saving language aids in the tradition of the great American hollow political apology. (A large-scale denial at the government or diplomatic level, by the way, is called a *dementi.)*

Some of the younger readership of my Wordwizard column may be contemplating a political career. Your probity is doubtless of the highest order, but against headline accusations you may find that a simple and brief self-defense will disappoint the public. You must know how to incorporate the following phraseology in your firm denial of any wrongdoing (preferably with a tone of wounded dignity, barely contained outrage, or grave disappointment, and of course with at least two members of your family standing at your side).

In making a graceful exit from political office, the substance of the farewell speech is not important. Its style and above all its windy self-justification and redundancy are what matters. It's a matter of using the appropriate rhetoric, of showing that one is above it all. For example, in a typical speech, one would not say simply, "I hereby deny the accusations." Rather, one would say, "I hereby deny, disavow, disaffirm, disallow, repudiate, dispute, reject, take issue with, refute, and absolutely renounce the accusations." The best legalese depends on such redundancies, and remember, many politicians are lawyers.

It's the language of self-excusing fustian, sort of an adroit turning the other cheek and patting oneself on the back at the same time.

The Five Dignified Conjunctions are *however, notwithstanding, moreover, of course,* and *furthermore.* Instead of simple and separate sentences (the literary, not the penal kind), work these in as connectives. However lame the content of what you are saying, these impart a stately tone and impress listeners.

The Twelve Emphatic Adverbs are *absolutely, categorically, unequivocally, utterly, completely, totally, thoroughly, clearly, vehemently, utterly and unequivocally, absolutely and categorically,* and *regrettably.* These intensives are invaluable, here and there, for asserting one's purity.

Above all, the Twenty Oil-of-Sanctity Phrases are the essence of any public self-defense speech. These twenty face-saving indispensables are *this vicious and unjustified attack, when all the facts come to light, let me just say this, in point of fact, as matter of fact, the fact of the matter is, by the same token, I'm well aware, as you are aware, come to a determination, my faith in our judicial system, to be perfectly frank, and so, disappointed in, after long and painful deliberation, pain and anguish to my family and friends, and so, will only further detract from the job at hand, I fully expect,* and *there's still important work to be done.*

In the practice of tail-between-the-legs face-saving, an exiting officeholder must for once take the high ground. His or her dudgeon cannot be high enough. Thus, while I am no political speechwriter, I humbly submit that this is the kind of resignation speech Woofton Assemblyman Peter Swatchman owed to his constituents:

"My fellow Wooftonians,

"As you are aware, certain vicious and unjustified attacks on my character have recently been made. Notwithstanding them, let me just say this. I want to state categorically that I clearly, vehemently, utterly, and unequivocally deny these smear tactics. The fact of the matter is that I am completely and, in point of fact, totally innocent of these fabrications. Moreover, I'm well aware that some people, regrettably, will go to any lengths to get at the truth. As a matter of fact, to be perfectly frank, I'm absolutely and categorically disappointed in these scurrilous charges, which furthermore will only detract from the job at hand. However, my unwavering faith in our judicial system remains absolutely unwavering. Furthermore, I fully expect that when all the facts have come to light, I will be thoroughly exonerated of these groundless accusations. And so, after long and painful deliberation, although there's still important work to be done, I have come to a determination that because of the pain and anguish to my beloved family and friends, I shall regretfully resign my position. At this juncture, of course, I have utterly and unequivocally, as well as absolutely and categorically, no further comment."

Even if you don't take up a political career, even a blameless one, these thirty-seven locutions are interesting as sine qua nons of political linguistic Americana. Embattled politicians never leave office without them.

The deliberately misspelled word in last week's column was *plebian*. It's *plebeian*.

FOWLERISMS

QUOTE OF THE WEEK: "If you can speak what you will never hear, if you can write what you will never read, you have done rare things."

—HENRY DAVID THOREAU

Can you guess the meanings of any of these ten terms: *anti-Saxonism, battered ornament, cannibalism, elegant variation, facetious formation, fetish, popularized technicality, slipshod extension, trailer style, walled-up object?*

You're probably pretty sure about cannibalism and fetish—but even there you'll be (in the context of this column) wrong. You should know the meaning of elegant variation, the subject of an earlier column. Is anti-Saxonism an early English racial attitude? Is a battered ornament a dented bauble? A popularized technicality an exploited loophole? Slipshod extension a form of male impotence? A walled-up object the victim in Poe's *The Cask of the Amontillado*?

Not in the slightest. These are all eternally useful critical terms—but as rarely seen as a whipoorwill—in the area of English usage, which is our area here.

We could call them useful out-of-use usage terms, but what they really are is Fowlerisms. They were coined or given permanency by the legendary and gentlemanly

English verbal vigilante Henry Watson Fowler (1858–1933) in his classic helpmate to good writing, *Modern English Usage.*

H. W. Fowler's book appeared in England in 1926, and ever since it has been irrevocably in print on both sides of the Atlantic as the writer's and editor's favorite reference companion—a very real companion rather than a mere guide because of its warmth, dry wit, and touches of eccentricity. To the end of his life Fowler remained a highly principled and hardworking but modest and charming scholar, and it is not surprising that *Modern English Usage,* covering some 450 items pertaining to English, from *a, an* to *-z-, -zz-,* is not only respected in its guidance but quite loved for its personal and often quirky flavor. (One quirk is Fowler's use throughout the book of the ampersand symbol, &, instead of the word *and.)*

However minor the subject under discussion, Fowler cared in the most genuine way about clarity, simplicity, and stylistic sanity. His book can always be turned to for advice on anything from comparatives and double passives to French borrowings and malaprops, or for some wisdom about specific troublesome words, such as *between* and *among* or *which* and *that.* Above all, he always firmly steers the reader away from resorting to any kind of pretension in speech or writing (among the book's entries are "Love of the Long Word," "Pedantry," and "Pomposities").

Certainly, some sections and aspects of *Modern English Usage* (sometimes known as MEU) are dated, British rather than American, or less relevant today. But as a whole the work is as fresh as it was when it was published.

Too often a name is legendary without many people knowing anything about the person. One note that Fowler wrote to the Oxford University Press late in his life tells us a lot about his selfless courage and wit. As a lexicographer working for that press, he was generously offered by his employer a servant so that he might give more attention to his lexical work. Fowler was sixty-eight. Declining the offer, he wrote back, as lexicographer Eric Partridge tells us:

"My half-hour from 7 to 7:30 this morning was spent in (1) a two-mile run along the road, (2) a swim in my next-door neighbour's pond. . . . That I am still in condition for such freaks I attribute to having for nearly thirty years no servants to reduce me to a sedentary and all-literary existence. And now you seem to say: Let us give you a servant, and the means of slow suicide and quick lexicography."

The ten terms mentioned above are proof that while *Modern English Usage* is a linguistic bible everybody should own, a number of Fowler's homemade terms remain unfamiliar. Most of us can talk easily enough about dangling participles, split infinitives, and euphemisms. But popularized technicalities?

This week let us take on some very helpful labels, courtesy of the great H.W.F., that can be indispensable in putting a handle on certain peculiarities and abuses of English.

Battered ornament is Fowler's broad term for any clichéd or hackneyed synonymous word or phrase used, where the simpler expression would be quite fine, for example, *walk down the aisle* instead of *marry* or *wed; the briny deep* instead of *the sea; the late great* instead of simply no modifier.

Battered ornaments are worn-out metaphors, "cute" expressions, archaic phrases, allusions intended to seem jocular or knowing, foreign words or idioms (when there are usable English equivalents), or even timeworn quotations—and more. (Fowler includes under his entry many cross-references, including "Hackneyed Phrases," "Sobriquets," "Vogue-Words," and "Worn-out Humour.") Broad though the application of the term may be, what all battered ornaments have in common is the writer's desire to show off a little and throw in a "literary" touch. The writer winks. The listener or reader winces.

A *cannibalism,* for Fowler, is not really a word that devours its own kind. Rather, it's an instance where a word—usually a preposition—gets left out (or eaten up) because it comes adjacent to another use of the word. An example would be the sentence *Charles is the one I have to make it up to smooth things over.* It should be *make it up to to smooth things over,* the second *to* having gotten lost in the shuffle. Or is it the first *to?*

If you've never particularly noticed such internal gulpings of prepositions in what you hear or read, it's kind of an interesting lapse to catch. A word related to Fowler's *cannibalism* is *haplograph,* which refers to an inadvertant omission of a syllable or word, for example, *a decision arrived at (at) noon,* where there should be two *at*'s. Its counterpart, the unintended doubling of a word or word element, is *dittograph,* for example, *how to get on on with them.* The haplograph and dittograph apply only to written English.

Elegant variation is a straining never to repeat the same unminor word. Thus, when a car becomes an *automobile,* then a *vehicle,* then a *conveyance* within the space of a few lines, the writer is taking the reader on an annoying prose ride. The perpetrator is trying to be colorful or trot out a rich vocabulary but usually succeeds only in confusing. Sportswriters, forever trying to enliven their reporting of a game, are possibly the worst culprits of synonym juggling.

A *facetious formation,* Fowler tells us, is any kind of made-up word concocted in a light or humorous vein, such as *absquatulate, underwhelmed, fantabulous,* and *supercalifragilisticexpialidocious.* Besides ludicrously long or mock-mistake words, Fowler includes in this category punning words *(infectionate),* mock Latin words *(hocus pocus),* blend or portmanteau words *(fishwich),* onomatopoeic words *(glug-glug),* and "irreverent familiarities" or facetious oaths *(criminy).* We need a good term for such antic inspirations that are so much a part of American idiom, going back to the pioneer days of tall tales.

A *fetish*, in linguistic terms, is a holding to a grammatical rule or a "correct" usage to a point that is excessive or mistaken—that is, refusing ever to split an infinitive (a faultily designated fault in English, as it is based on making English word order behave like that of Latin), to end a sentence with a preposition (otherwise known as an Addisonian termination), or to use a particular noun or verb twice within the same sentence. Believing that there are hard and fast rules governing all cases for choosing between *which* and *that* is also a fetish, as is pedantry about certain spellings of foreign-origin words. Fetishes are often the sacred cows of purists, who refuse to budge in these matters and who generally are ignorant of historical precedents in the English language. But most of us have a fetish or two and cherish it, guaranteeing that contention about English usage will always be kept alive.

A *popularized technicality* is any term that originally—and in its purest sense—had a technical or profession-related meaning but that has become a vogue word. *Parameter*, which comes from mathematics, and *segue*, from television jargon, are prime examples, but popularized technicalities are countless in English. From astrology to zoology, words get borrowed, exposed—and often blunted or changed in meaning—and acquire a cachet that makes them fashionable. Fowler notes many words now considered quite mainstream that were once scientific, professional, or academic, including *complex, optimism, devil's advocate, asset, flamboyant, to the nth, eliminate, myth,* and *hectic*.

Related to the above is *slipshod extension,* Fowler's coined label for what happens to a word's meaning when it gets appropriated by the masses, or what is "likely to occur when some accident gives currency among the uneducated to words of learned origin." It is not so much a broadening as a warping of meaning from thoughtless overuse, as has been the case with *dilemma, special pleading, decimate,* and *viable.* Our utterance is ever awash in slipshod extension, and we're all now and then contributing to it. It's maybe regrettable but quite unstoppable.

The person who writes tiresome long sentences that seem about to come to an end but then continue on is one who writes *trailers,* a style that to Fowler "is perhaps of all styles the most exasperating." You probably know one or two people who write or talk in this way, as if reluctant ever to reach that punctuation point called a period. (These vapid chains of clauses and afterthoughts have also been known as accordion sentences or decapitable sentences.) Fowler gives several British examples of such ongoing, going-on sentences, but they are too painful to read or reproduce here.

Our books, newspapers, and periodicals are chock full of compound sentence constructions that cheat by omitting a word or two, but we'll only know enough to call this phenomenon a *walled-up object* if we consult the great Fowler. The sentence *The manager scolded and ordered her to the bench* should better be *The manager scolded her and ordered her to the bench.* Likewise, *We had to count and change the bills into coins* should be *We had to count the bills and change them into coins.* Look familiar? This kind of sloppiness or abusive space-saving happens when two verbs used together have different follow-up needs; they can't quite legitimately team up with the same object. (When a compressing or yoking is done for a clever, two-senses-of-the-same-word effect—for example, *The lazy handyman cleaned up his act and her windows as well*—it's called syllepsis or sometimes zeugma.)

Finally, there is Fowler's *anti-Saxonism.*

English, as you should know, has a rich vocabulary drawn from both simple and clear "original" or Saxon words and Latin. For example, Saxon and Latin counterparts are, respectively, *foreword* and *preface, happen* and *transpire, beg* and *importune.*

Just as *Saxonism* is Fowler's word for a zealous belief in favoring, using, or digging up etymologically native words, anti-Saxonism is a writer's propensity to avoid the simple and clear word and use instead Latinate synonyms, which are typically words of more than one syllable that sound a little more intellectual. Jargon of all stripes abounds today, and most of it, avoiding plain concrete words for pretentious abstract ones, is anti-Saxonism.

These ten Fowlerisms are indeed technical terms. But like so many other technical terms, they denote usages in English that are everyday, general, and perennial.

The deliberately misspelled word in last week's column was *violincello*. It's *violoncello*.

PROFLATITUDES

WORD OF THE WEEK: *calembour*—a pun

QUOTE OF THE WEEK: "Words, like eyeglasses, blur everything that they do not make clear."

—JOSEPH JOUBERT

"Hopefully we know what we have to do. We have to play up to our capabilities as a team."

Can you sling this kind of English? If you plan to become a famous professional athlete in America, it's time to learn how to talk like one. So here's a little test for you or yours. What are the expected answers to the following typical sports-reporter baseball questions? (Correct answers follow.)

1. What do you consider your role to be on the team this year?
2. Are you concerned about the team's losing streak (or being four games behind)?
3. Any idea what went wrong in today's loss?
4. It must be frustrating—another game your team probably should have won.
5. Can you say enough about————, who again won the game for you?
6. What are you most proud of about your season this year?

7. What can you do to beat your opponents, who are so heavily favored?
8. How did you manage to beat them?
9. Any idea why the press has come down so hard on you?
10. How do you feel about the tragic bungee-jumping death of your two teammates in the off season?

When it comes to sports and athletes, silence, once golden, is now more olden than golden. And in its place we have proflatitudes. They are not only dribbling relentlessly out of our home TV speakers, they are depressingly abroad among fans in our humble town of Woofton. They are coming out of the mouths of babes.

What is a proflatitude? It's a pat and hackneyed statement by a sports star that is painfully predictable. There is the general cliché and the general platitude, but a proflatitude—now epidemic in our age of mass-media sports—is a soberly trite remark long overdue for retirement. It is a proflatitude because it is dispensed regularly by interview-numb *pro*fessional athletes and because it is a fake or empty *pro*fundity about his or her sport. It is, flatly, flat.

A proflatitude is often preceded by the word *hopefully*. This is a good thing to know, a kind of cue that yet another one is on the way.

One thing the virus of proflatitudes tells us is that maybe we could do with less attention to professional sports in America. Nowadays, of course, it is sacrilegious to suggest this.

You won't find *proflatitude* in your dictionary. It's making its season opener, as a term, here in this column. If we can't fight or stop something unfortunate, we can at least label it (and maybe touch a little on the traits of what has been dubbed *sportspeak*).

If proflatitudes remained on the playing field, we could breathe easier. But because of their absorbtion by so many sports fans from watching television, they're also being airily thrown about by amateur couch-potato fans, young and old.

Time was when spectator sports weren't multimillion-dollar industries. There was little logorrhea, less pseudopunditry. To listen to a baseball game forty years ago was a gentle pleasure. There was one announcer and the soothing and even hypnotic sound of the crowd in the background, a gentle surf to the ears that would occasionally erupt into a roar but always subside again. The announcing wasn't always in impeccable English (nor should it have been), but the talk wasn't manically continuous.

Those days are gone, even on the radio. Television and its dictates loom over all the big sports. Despite the visual dimension it offers that radio lacks, there seems to be more audio than ever. It is not a blessing. The price for watching or listening to a baseball, football, basketball, or hockey game is having to endure continual jockorrhea.

As Edwin Newman noted some years ago, "There is no way to measure the destructive effect of sports broadcasting on ordinary American English, but it must be considerable. In the early days sports broadcasting was done, with occasional exceptions such as Clem McCarthy, by non-experts, announcers. Their knowledge of the sports they described varied, but their English was generally of a high order. If they could not tell you much about the inside of the game they were covering, at any rate what they did tell you you could understand." Then, Newman says, along came the experts—the former athletes.

The term *sportspeak* was coined a few years ago by journalist Robert Lipsyte. Print journalism was what Lipsyte was applying the word to chiefly, but sportspeak is also by now inescapable on TV. Sportspeak, or sportsese as it has also been called, is the breezy, self-consciously "colorful," and pumped-up jargon that typifies accounts of games. There is the basic play-by-play reporting, of course, but around and through it swirl ever-varied verbs ("he really hammered that one"), as much "colorful" slang as possible ("that homer was a clothesline express"), humorous sobriquets ("they don't call him the Enforcer for nothing"), expressions of awestruck amazement ("the greatest catch I've seen all year"), and all in all an endless resort to metaphors and clichéd phrases. To say nothing, of course, of some bad grammar and considerable misuse of words (but without the charm of Dizzy Dean's famous solecisms).

Particularly in baseball sportspeak, sportscasters have unofficial roles to play. The role of the play-by-play announcer is (1) to eradicate silence; (2) to sound crisply well informed; (3) and to say as frequently as humanly possible "No question about it" or "No doubt about it." Nowadays he has a partner or co-anchor, the colorcaster. The colorcaster is usually a former player and must know the right things to interject in particular game situations; be able to throw in statistical facts, however meaningless they are essentially; and know how to exaggerate effortlessly. But above all, the role of the colorcaster is (1) to know when to sound amazed and excited; (2) to have a fund of colorful-sounding metaphors; (3) to chortle now and then like a game guy; and (4) —how do they do it—to report to the fans, by unquestioned telepathy, just exactly what catchers, pitchers, batters, and managers are feeling or thinking any moment during the game.

What about the role of the player when he is interviewed? It is chiefly (1) to emphasize team success as being the only thing important to him; (2) to appear modest in referring to his own abilities; (3) to mention that he values a leadership role or just wants to contribute; and (4) to use the word *hopefully* before anything he says to make sure it's not spontaneous or fresh.

How did sportspeak come into being? Simply and quite naturally from the worthy attempt to make more lively the routine facts and results of games. English is a wonderfully rich language. Why not use it to make sports coverage as readable or hearable as it can be?

Even the great sportswriter—and great writer—Red Smith defended sportspeak, "outside of the fact that sportspeak is used by too many who know nothing of sports."

Or maybe by sports fans who like to think they know sports.

What about when it's parroted—along with proflatitudes—by nonathletes who like to think they know everything about sports?

Sportspeak may always have its place. But thanks to telecasting's seeming horror of more than three consecutive seconds of silence, more nonsense, clichés, and pseudoprofundities are being sent out over the airwaves than you can shake a microphone at. Besides proflatitudes, we also have statistics and pseudostatistics. We have countless *hopefully*s and *good success*es (as opposed to *bad successes*). And with half of the "sports" news these days treating of the business (greed) and penal (drugs or after-hours misdemeanors) aspects of a given sport, even fans are glibly throwing around talk about comparative salaries, agent negotiations, contract extensions, litigation between owners and players' unions, and the latest lapse of a player who is a serial drug rehabilitant.

At a local Woofton luncheonette of late I recently heard a hot legalistic discussion of free agency, the passing of waivers, the exercise of options, and a team having to "eat" some star's contract. The voices were rather treble. I turned around to see not four local contract-law attorneys but three boys and one girl wearing Woofton High School jackets.

Sportspeak is spreading. As part of America's self-engulfing pop culture, it has become a ready-made lingo for anybody wanting to sound like an expert. And for their numbing predictability and often downright hypocrisy, proflatitudes are the worst part of sportspeak.

How do you fight these ready-made sports banalities? By never uttering one. You have to learn to recognize them. You have to know the classic proflatitudes that just keep on coming as remorselessly as "Have a nice day!"

In the delightful minor-league-baseball movie *Bull Durham*, a brief scene on a bus shows the older player teaching the young pitcher the clichés he must master for future interviews: (1) "We gotta play 'em one game at a time"; (2) "I'm just happy to be here, hope I can help the ball club"; and (3) "I just want to give it my best shot, and the good Lord willing, things will work out."

These are Mr. Wordwizard's Top Ten Proflatitudes— or the correct proflatitudinous answers to the ten questions above:

What do you consider your role to be on the team this year?

A leader in the clubhouse, off the field as well as on. (Or) I'm just glad to be here, and I just want to contribute and have good success.

Are you concerned about the team's losing streak (or being four games behind)?

We just have to take it one game at a time.

Any idea what went wrong in today's loss?

We just didn't execute—not to take anything away from our opponents. (Or) We just didn't get the job done. (Or) We were out there giving 110 percent—we just came up short.

It must be frustrating—another game your team probably should have won.

The breaks just haven't been going our way—not to take anything away from our opponents. (Or) No doubt about it—we've been struggling.

Can you say enough about————, who again won the game for you?

He's just a guy who does all those little things that never show up in the box score. He has all the tools and has taken it to another level. (Or) He did a super job.

What are you most proud of about your season this year?

I've had some good success and put up some pretty good

numbers. I always try to give 110 percent, step up when it counts, and stay within myself.

What can you do to beat your opponents, who are so heavily favored?

We know we have our backs to the wall, but we just have to stay focused and play the way we know we can play, play our game. (Or) *We just have to play up to our capabilities.*

How did you manage to beat them?

We managed to put it all together. (Or) *They did a lot of talking, we just came to play.*

Any idea why the press has come down so hard on you?

It's of course the New York media.

How do you feel about the tragic bungee-jumping death of your two teammates in the off season?

Injuries are part of the game, but it's the kind of thing that puts sports in proper perspective.

This, of course, is only an introductory sampling of proflatitudes. We could add *After this loss, it'll be a long plane ride home; I was in a zone* (of performance excellence); *I've been struggling and pressing;* and the inescapable-on-the-airwaves *No question about it.* And remember, nobody can master proflatitudese without using the *-wise* suffix every ten or so words, as in *gamewise, effortwise, successwise, schedulewise, leadershipwise,* and *role-modelwise.* You have to give 110 percent—never 100—so that those sportscasters will repeatedly *allude to* (never *mention*) you as a *class act.* You have to be, you know, *proflatitudewise.*

The deliberately misspelled word in last week's column was *whipoorwill.* It's *whippoorwill.*

HOPEFULLY—NOT

Word of the Week: *abecedarian*—pertaining to the alphabet or elementary

Quote of the Week: "All good writing is *swimming under water* and holding your breath."

—F. Scott Fitzgerald

The real trouble with *that* word has not been revealed until now.

Your language-listening assignment for this week is to wear your wristwatch and go to any organizational meeting, lunchroom, locker room, or other place where chat is going on. Then time how many minutes pass before somebody uses the word *hopefully*.

Actually, you might bring a stopwatch rather than a wristwatch.

Along with cacophonous video games and ultrabaggy clothing, that controversial word has reached fair Woofton, and she is its. Except that much of the resistance to *hopefully* is long gone. The battle has been lost. The new free-floating use of the word is here to stay, not only in Woofton but across America.

Feelings still run so hot and high about *hopefully* that, to many purists, the issue is the quickest litmus test for determining who cares about English and who doesn't —the test that separates the higher minds and the lower beings.

The new sense of *hopefully,* if you need reminding, is not that of *with hope,* as in *They listened to the weather forecast hopefully,* but that of *it is to be hoped,* as in *Hopefully, we'll hear the weather forecast soon.* In the first instance the word is a simple adverb, modifying a verb. In the latter-day-and-here-to-stay instance it has become a modifier for a whole clause or sentence, a kind of floating, broad-brush adverb that does not especially refer to the speaker's hopes.

You'll be fortunate to hear the word used in its older, traditional way anywhere today. A 1985 *New York Times* editorial containing the sentence *Tommy Herr, player representative of the St. Louis Cardinals, hopefully finds that many ballplayers are getting "tired of protecting drug users" and may drop their opposition to the testing* was worth cutting out and saving for this reason. The line now seems an antiquated memento. There's little hope that Americans will be using the word like this, as a plain verb modifier, much in the near future.

The craze for abusing *hopefully* began in the 1960s. Nobody knows exactly where the virus came from, although different explanations have been offered. One is that using the word impersonally to mean "it is to be hoped" was inspired by the German word *hoffentlich.* This is dubious, not least of all because German also has a separate word meaning "full of hope," *hoffnungsvoll.* Others have ventured that the usage slipped into English by way of, variously, Dutch, Yiddish, or Pennsylvania Dutch, but with no evidence.

It's my theory that it was brought here as a contagious brain-softener by aliens before they began their abductions of and experiments on human beings.

In any case, the rage for this term provoked rage, hisses, and howls of protest. The issue continues to be a battleground—there'll never be a concensus—but most of the eminent language-watchers and columnists who condemned the new usage in the 1970s have openly changed their open minds and said we must learn to live with it and love it. The first British "misuses" of *hope-*

fully date (in the *Oxford English Dictionary*) to 1970. Yes, it seems we passed the virus on to them. On the other hand, the growing use of the word notwithstanding, the Usage Panel of the *American Heritage Dictionary* has become less accepting over the years. In 1969, 44 percent allowed it; in 1975, 37 percent; and in 1988, only 27 percent.

So what is wrong with using *hopefully* in the same way that we use *surely, happily, strangely, ideally, sadly,* and *mercifully,* all adverbs that can be used both as adverb modifiers and sentence modifiers (as opposed to *luckily, fortunately,* and *certainly,* which are mostly used as sentence modifiers)? Admittedly (to use another word that could be added to the latter grouping), there are justifying precedents or analogies for *hopefully* here.

Defenders also argue that its popularity today only attests to its usefulness. They say it fills a need because there is no exact substitute; the alternative expressions *it is to be hoped* or *one hopes* are longer and stiffer and, some think, don't have quite the same meaning. Perhaps the best defense is that of novelist Cathleen Schine, in only eight words: *"Hopefully* means 'God willing' in a secular world." The very depersonalizing of who is doing the hoping is, she says, a good thing for our language. It "is a word full of hope."

Hope schmope. I might agree if the word hadn't become a standard throat-clearing expression.

Hopefully-haters, on the other hand, think the word "strains *-ly* to the breaking point" (M. Stanley Whitley) and that its epidemic popularity will "infect" the meanings of other adverbs—as it apparently has the word *thankfully.* And we don't use *hopelessly* this way, do we —yet? The haters feel that its lack of point of view (that is, who, exactly or presumptuously, is the hoper) is a bad thing, not a good thing.

But what sticks in the craw most about *hopefully* is that it is a vogue word—actually, one that has gone far beyond being a mere vogue word and become a veritable communicational tic for happily (or *hopefully*) afflicted Americans. The deplorable thing about *hopefully* is not grammatical or semantic, it's psychological.

Let me count the ways.

You see, *hopefully* has become a mental knee-jerk word, or rather an unmental one. It's become a posturing lead-off, a by-now unconscious one. As a sentence detergent, it's a cliché that pops out with almost any statement, no longer just with those genuinely involving any real investment of hope. So its use is often not earned, and it usually has as much meaning as a cheap coloring agent.

The color is the color of aw-shucks modesty, if not of false modesty or false humility. People like to put the word before any kind of remark to give it a nice flavor. Why say *He'll never notice I overcharged him* when you can sound much nicer by saying *Hopefully, he won't notice that I've overcharged him?*

Being floatingly impersonal, the new *hopefully* is also a cop-out from the good old-fashioned subjective. It's psychologically evasive. The "I" has no responsibility. It's merely a matter of "Gosh, with luck it'll turn out for humble me that . . ."—making the usage yet another signpost of passivity (or quasi-victimization) rather than of active, direct, personal speech. It's another subtle squirt of the passive voice in our couch-potato age—not the vital active voice—into whatever follows or surrounds it. It's being nice and careful, carefully nice, aw-shucks upbeat, one of the good guys.

Literary scholar Benjamin DeMott has remarked that the new empty-calorie *hopefully* is an attempt at "impression management," a kind of emotional sanitizing: "I'm saying that I connect *hopefully* with a certain paint-out-the-unpleasantness attitude toward life—with hope that's too easy, too manipulative, too clearly an instrument of what the new anthropologists contentedly call 'impression management.'"

Its overuse bespeaks laziness, as do all overused expressions. How many brainwashed *hopefully*-ites ever bother to consider alternative expressions, such as *let's hope, ideally, with luck, optimally, knock on wood, if things work out, if I'm (we're) lucky, if fortune smiles on me (us),* or the good, old-fashioned *God willing?*

The new *hopefully* is the product of too many people seeing, via television, too many people trying to strike a note of sincerity "on the record"—while being interviewed. The word is perfect for any celebrity attempting to seem self-effacing or any pro athlete affecting to be just a humble part of the team.

In short, *hopefully* is the perfect cosmetic adverb to give a tone of humble uplift to any utterance however banal and to make it insufferably more banal. Some people use words to impress. Some can now rely on *hopefully* with scarcely a thought—it's by now too unconscious a speech fixture always to be premeditated—to remind others how impressively nice they are.

It's the "Have a nice day" adverb.

Reasons schmeasons, here's a little secret to keep in mind. The reason many "strict" language-lovers will refuse to use a certain fashionable expression is *not at all* for reasons of grammar, history, meaning, or etymology. It's because they know, like your Aunt Sophie the balabusta, where the word has *been.*

The deliberately misspelled word in last week's column was *absorbtion.* It's *absorption.*

THE NONSENSE
WE ALL SPEAK

WORD OF THE WEEK: *disedification*—offending religious or moral values

QUOTE OF THE WEEK: "Eating words has never given me indigestion."

—WINSTON CHURCHILL

Some expressions, as we say, *come in handy.* But why just come in handy? Shouldn't they also go out handy?

My intent this week is to pique (or even peak) your curiosity about phrases that you utter all the time—and that make no literal or logical sense. If you're feeling listless, you're in luck, as the latter part of the column will be a list.

Do you realize that we all speak semantically weird phrases to each other every day and never give it a second thought? That's because we're all, in a sense, idioms idiots. Which is to say, whatever the English language is, it's not logical or consistent.

What do the phrases *get one's second wind, the world round, a crying shame, sit in on,* and *hot under the collar* have in common?

In a word (to use another example of this phenomenon), they are idioms. Some letters I've received of late have complained about English usage when it is "illogical," so that a little discussion of idioms is in order (to use another idiom).

The word *idiom,* from the Greek, means in its broad sense the manner of verbal expression—or "language style"—of a whole group of people, and it can also be used to denote the characteristic style of quality of any mode of expression, including music. But in a nuts-and-bolts discussion of language, an idiom is a particular but traditional expression, an idiosyncrasy ingrained in the language.

Idioms, from A to Z (to use a common idiom), are phrases peculiar to a language. They are indeed peculiar, usually, because they are not necessarily logical, predictable, or grammatical, and the meaning of the Greek word that *idiom* is derived from is essentially "peculiarity." Meaning in English is not always literal. Sometimes it's idiomatic and defies analysis. Some idioms are metaphorical, but others are not, and when analyzed word by word, they don't exactly make sense. But they are idioms because they are ensconced in the language, having grown over a long enough period of time to make them invulnerable, unchangeable.

They shouldn't be tampered with or "corrected," however quirky they seem. If the idiom goes *to move heaven and earth,* do not decide it would sound better as *to move the heavens and the earth.* Making one word a plural and adding two definite articles are minor changes, but it is precisely such minor changes that must never be forced upon tried-and-true idioms. It's *at cross-purposes,* not *at crossed purposes,* and it's *the die is cast,* not *the dice are cast.*

Not surprisingly, then, when we say something is idiomatic, we mean that it is natural and conveys a definite meaning, not that it is stiltedly correct.

Idioms are like odd articles of hand-me-down clothing. Upon inspection they're a little strange, but the wearer quickly becomes used to them and scarcely gives them a thought. The idiom, we might say, is language's way of showing that, semantically, the whole is greater than—or different from—the sum of the parts. Idioms are also, Walter Savage Landor said, "the life and spirit of language."

Prepositions (or what usage authority Theodore Bernstein calls verb tails) are key elements in many idioms. For example, we find fault in a person (noun) but we find fault with him (pronoun). There is usually no rhyme or reason why a given expression uses an *in* rather than a *to* or an *about* rather than an *upon*. It's just the way the idiom evolved. It is ordained by what scholar Otto Jesperson calls "that tyrannical, capricious, utterly incalculable thing, idiomatic usage."

Many of us also associate the word *idiom* with learning a foreign language—learning the idioms is the toughest part, with the possible exception of pronunciation. Whatever the tongue, idioms are usually the real stumbling blocks. The only thing to do is to memorize them, cross one's fingers, and try to use them. They are always traps for a foreigner, and getting them wrong can immediately expose somebody who is not a native speaker. Need a good military password in wartime to confound a foreign enemy? You could do worse than to choose a line including a common English idiom that is slightly illogical or ungrammatical—say, "The witch is weighed every which way but when."

So idioms are a central and interesting phenomenon in our language (or any language), one, because they're so indispensable; and two, because their wording is permanent and unchangeable and shouldn't be meddled with. What, for example, does *to have a good mind to* do something have to do with having a good mind? But you dasn't modify the wording to, say, *to have a justifiable inclination to* do something. By their very nature, idioms are givens in a language. They have a certain sense, and they do not give.

Sense?

Kind of curious, when you think about it, that hundreds of phrases we rely on to get our meanings across don't exactly make sense when we think about them. Or maybe it's more curious that we don't think about it. Or yet more curious that we all understand what each other is saying perfectly well.

If you grew up in this country, you presumably speak English with some ease. Yet it could fairly be said (to borrow another idiom) that all your life you've airily uttered phrases that don't make literal, logical, or grammatical sense. To *climb down* a ladder? How do you climb down something? To *put up with* somebody? Where do you put them up, unless in a hotel? A *near miss*? Shouldn't that be a near hit? To *put somebody on*? On what, if not a train? A *point well taken*? Shouldn't it be a *point well made*?

In French the adjective often comes the noun after, like a sign hung on its back. In German the verbs usually at the end of the sentence go. In English we're much more sensible—except for hundreds of out-of-kilter idioms. They're like certain spellings: The more you stare at them, the stranger they seem. It's like walking or like riding a bicycle—natural, until you stop and try to analyze it.

Well, we're going to climb off the bicycle briefly.

Here, to prove that we continually utter literal nonsense without giving it a thought, are quite a few common English idioms for your momentary consideration. I lack the space to go into their explanations or geneologies. (A whole column could be spent on any one or two of them.) If your curiosity is aroused, this is an opportunity for you to do a little theorizing or research yourself. The letters I receive make it sadly clear that too few Wooftonians even bother to make use of a good dictionary. For these idioms, our Woofton Public Library and our local bookstores both have numerous books on phrase origins.

If a foreigner learning English asked you how in the world any of these idioms make any kind of literal *sense*, could you shed some light on the matter? In particular, could you explain the underlined part of each one listed below?

under the weather
to have *words* with
fit as a *fiddle*
to *give* the lie to
to have *a* nerve
to take something *up* with
to *do* someone proud
to *take it out* on
dead as a *doornail*
to have a *good mind* to
to *stretch* a point
as right as *rain*
through *and through*
to sleep like a *top*
to do right *by*
to *put up* with
head over heels
to *put one on*
for the *most* part
to be taken to *task*
to *go* (one) one better
the *same difference*
to wash *up*
to fix *up*
in no *wise*
no great *shakes*
to make both *ends* meet
to luck *out*
far and away
off the *wall*
going great *guns*
to *have it in* for
all *get-out*
to *hit it off*
by and large
to hope *against hope*
to give one *away*
hand over fist
to come into *one's own*

to turn the *tables* on
up to *scratch*
wouldn't *put it past* you
at *large*
better *off*
cracked up to be
to point *up* (something)
their name is *legion*
in one's *salad* days
to knock for a *loop*
of late
to *bring to heel*
by *fits and starts*
to *knock it off*
to have one's *moments*
out of the question
spoiling for a fight
to *take it out on*
long in *the tooth*
just as *well*
to whoop it *up*
to have one's wits *about* him
to think *the world* of
to go *whole hog*
to *dress down*
to *stand down*
most all
quite a few
to *beat the band*
to rain *cats and dogs*
to fall *between* the cracks
bold as *brass*
to *fly in the face* of
to get along *famously*
to *center around*
to see if one *can't*
to get *the better of*

as *good* as (dead, finished, etc.)
to *pull* a long face
to get one's *goat*
to get *the hang* of
to be *hard put*
to *hang fire*
to *seize up*
to *go* somebody one better
under way
like as not

touch and go
time and again
in its own *right*
to *shift* for oneself
to not *hold* with
in a *pig's eye*
cracked up to be
sell (someone) *a bill of goods*
out of *whack*
take your life in *your own hands*

Again, if you're interested in learning the origins of these and other odd expressions, you'll find countless books on phrase derivations at the library and in bookstores. Be forewarned that for every one "explanation" for an idiom, there's often another, different explanation. Meanwhile, keep in mind that we all continue to utter nonsensical expressions day in and day out. But what in the world does *day out* mean?

The deliberately misspelled word in last week's column was *concensus*. It's *consensus*.

LOST POSITIVES

WORD OF THE WEEK: *psittacism*—boring, repetitive, parrot-like speech

QUOTE OF THE WEEK: "To me, the greatest pleasure of writing is not what it's about, but the inner music that words make."

—TRUMAN CAPOTE

Except maybe for howling malapropisms and rare good puns, there's no language sport that can so quickly bring a smile to a witful person as devising lost positives.

Historically, it's sometimes the negative that endures or prevails in the vocabulary of English. Our dictionaries include many words beginning with *non-, in-, un-, dis-,* and *mis-,* for which we will find no affirmative counterparts. For example, today we have *uncouth* but no *couth.*

Couth is a lost positive.

The English word-stock, unfortunately, does not operate by a system of checks and balances. Because there is a word *dismayed* does not ensure that there will be a word *mayed*—or that both will be used enough to survive down through the years.

Still, the simple logic of it nags at us when we think about it. (This column is dedicated to making you think about it.) If *non-, in-, un-, dis-,* and *mis-* are mere combining forms in our familiar Latinate English words, it makes good sense that the words they get attached to should exist in their own right. They often do—or did. The non-*non* counterparts don't gain currency sometimes somehow. They become obsolete, to be tracked down only in the great but slightly dusty chifferobe of the *Oxford English Dictionary*.

Once-existent or not, these embodied positives fascinate many people who like to play with words or to make up new ones. In this case, to find the new coinage only a little syllable subtraction is required. Who can resist this game?

We could well call these amusing coinages ghost counterparts. Or phantonyms. But the term they've been known by, at least in recent years, is lost positives. Almost fifty years ago columnist John Crosby facetiously organized the Society for the Restoration of Lost Positives, as usage authority William Morris reports. His put-on, prefix-offing club may no longer be extant (that is, it may be tant), but delight in lost positives keeps rearing its headlessness.

A close relative to the lost positive is what is called a back-formation, which is not a spinal growth. A back-formation is a word that is created, or that comes into being, by "subtracting" what seems to be a prefix or suffix from another, longer word; for example, making *burgle* from *burglar* and *one-up* from *one-upmanship*. It's a natural, if unceremonious, way of creating a new word, a handy forming of, say, a verb where only a noun exists. Not all attempted back-formations "stick" (or stick around) in English, and quite a few do not receive a warm reception from language purists—such as *buttle* from *butler*. But among those that have survived are *enthuse* (from *enthusiasm*), *peeve* (from *peevish*), *reminisce* (from *reminiscence*), *diagnose* (from *diagnosis*), *grovel* (from *groveling*), *peddle* (from *peddler*), *televise* (from *television*), *drowse* (from *drowsy*), *edit* (from *editor*), *locate* (from *location*), *commute* (from *commutation*), *emote* (from *emotion*), *baby-sit* (from *baby-sitter*), *donate* (from *donation*), *process* (from *procession*), and *reclusion* (from *recluse*). Many back-formations, as you can see, are verbs, but anything is possible in this phenomenon of word-form adaptation.

The lost positive is like the back-formation in being a kind of creative subtraction, but it is a facetious kind of coinage. It is not a forming of a different part of speech but rather a kind of whimsical inverting or reversal of a current word. Venturing a lost positive is a kind of mischievous equal-opportunity exercise with words

Lost positives are rare creatures, little eye-openers. If *dismantled,* what exactly would *mantled* mean? How many *de-* words yield good lost positives?

Here the prefix should always have a negating or opposite-making sense. The common *in-,* for instance, sometimes means "not" or "non" but not always. Should any prefixed words be fair game for making lost positives?

I think not. To be a true lost positive, the one word it has been derived from should be quickly recognizable. For example, deriving from the word *mischief* the word *chief* just doesn't work. The connection isn't readily evident. Readers will likely raise their eyebrows in puzzlement rather than smile (the test of any lost positive). The same is true of *indent, dislocate, nonstick, decant,* and *deform.* The lost positive has to have a certain look, a naked or odd look, *as if something were missing,* which of course it is and which can be quickly supplied—aha! —by the reader's positive- and negative-charged mind.

One key to recognizing a candidate for a lost positive is this: The main body (or "positive" part) of the given word will be unusual, in that you usually won't be able to think of any other word of which that element is a part; for example, *unscathed,* there being no such other word as *disscathed, hyperscathed,* and so on.

English teachers (and language columnists) should not hesitate to let their students (and readers) play with lost positives, for two reasons. First, fooling around with the game of lost positives will teach anybody much about the origins of words. Was a particular present-day word once an Old English word? Does it come from Latin? Was it borrowed at some point from French? Getting a feeling for how a word "divides" is crucial here—and it's easy to be mistaken. Devising or discovering lost positives thus fosters an awareness of word elements in English, those affixes and combining forms. When so few students today learn any Latin, which is invaluable for comprehending English vocabulary, a basic sense of word parts is at least some help.

Second, the search for lost positives can quickly lead anybody into a dictionary, never a bad thing.

Even Australians, Mr. Morris relates in his *Harper Dictionary of Contemporary Usage,* enjoy lost positives, as evidenced by this letter to an American news magazine: "The Society for the Preservation of Titheses commends your ebriated and scrutable use of delible and defatigable, which are gainly, sipid, and couth. We are gruntled and consolate that you have the ertia and eptitude to choose such putably pensible titheses, which we parage."

More recently, in *The New Yorker,* writer Jack Winter eptly mixed quite a promptu, called-for, and sipid salad of lost positives in a gainly one-page piece he entitled "How I Met My Wife." Rather than the full cerpt, here is an excerpt: "I was plussed. It was concerting to see that she was communicado, and it nerved me that she was interested in a pareil like me, sight seen. Normally, I had a domitable spirit, but, being corrigible, I felt capacitated—as if this were something I was great shakes at—and forgot that I had succeeded in situations like this only a told number of times. So, after a terminable delay, I acted with mitigated gall and made my way through the ruly crowd with strong givings."

But do keep in mind that concocting lost positives is not only entertaining. It can also be positively instructive if a little research—into the *Oxford English Dictionary*—goes along with it. You'll learn whether a particular lost positive ever really was once a word, for example. If it wasn't, you'll probably discover that your sense of how the current word was formed is mistaken. All in all, you'll improve your knowledge of word origins.

And what better way to start than by ending here with a little quiz on lost positives?

Which lost positives, in the following list, do you think are or were at one time, in the history of the English language, genuine words (findable in the *Oxford English Dictionary*)? If you think the deducted word *after* the parentheses does or did exist, note down a yes. If you think not, note down a no. Answers follow.

(un)couth
(dis)sheveled
(un)kempt
(in)sidious
(in)nocuous
(in)ept
(in)ane
(non)descript
(in)digent
(im)pecunious
(in)vidious
(in)delible
(in)ertia
(dis)consolate
(in)scrutable
(dis)maying
(dis)turb
(non)plus
(dis)combobulate
(in)effable
(in)exorable

(in)finity
(in)fidel
(in)genuous
(dis)mantle
(dis)illusionment
(dis)traught
(in)alienable
(un)witting
(un)earth
(un)scathed
(un)wieldy
(non)sequitur
(de)celerate
(de)fective
(de)ficient
(de)molition
(de)tach
(de)terrent
(mis)anthrope
(over)whelm

The rooting out of lost affirmatives should never be thought of as a feckless pursuit. It can have quite a bit of feck. Always think positive.

The deliberately misspelled word in last week's column was *geneology*. It's *genealogy*.

Answers to Lost Positives Quiz:

yes (couth)
yes (sheveled)
yes (kempt)
no
yes (nocuous)
no
no
yes (descript)
no
yes (pecunious)
no
yes (delible)
no
yes (consolate)
yes (scrutable)
no
no
no
no
yes (effable)
yes (exorable)

yes (finity)
no
no
yes (mantle)
no
no
yes (alienable)
yes (witting)
yes (earth)
yes (scathed)
yes (wieldy)
yes (sequitur)
no
no
no
yes (molition)
no
no
no
yes (whelm)

FOR SWEARING OR FORSWEARING

WORD OF THE WEEK: *juvenilia*—a writer's youthful works

QUOTE OF THE WEEK: "A word is not the same with one writer as with another. One tears it from his guts. The other pulls it out of his overcoat pocket."

—CHARLES PEGUY

Could you use a few new—or old—and refreshingly different names to call people? Admit it, you do have occasion to call people names.

This is a family publication, but the everyday speech I've been hearing around Woofton—well. I'm talking about speech of the intemperate variety. At a heated argument I witnessed in a store last week, a customer was so enraged by the saleswoman that all she could sputter was "You . . . you . . . !" (In old books, it's usually "Why, you . . . you . . . !") She couldn't fill in the blanks.

But most Wooftonians, particularly younger ones, have no trouble filling in the blanks. Frustration or anger can be an occasion to characterize the person responsible, but while provokers and occasions and circumstances vary greatly, those same old scurrilous epithets seem to tumble out.

I count eleven standby epithets.

Three begin with *s,* two with *b,* two with *c,* one with *p,* one with *m,* one with *d,* and one with *a.* (You'll have to fill in the blanks.) To curse somebody out, an aroused utterer will often use these in combination or one or more of six equally worn-out modifiers: (you) *dirty* ———, *filthy* ———, *rotten* ———, *stinking* ———, *raving* ———, or *flaming* ———. Other here-unprintable adjectives are easily and eternally derived from the eleven nouns.

You may have noticed that these little strings of profanity don't usually make much sense. Yet paradoxically, you can be sure that the name-caller means every adjective, noun, and double-noun he or she says.

Then there's the two-syllable *a*-word, literally for a posterior orifice, which won't be spelled out here.

An a——— is a contemptible person, contemptible for being either manifestly stupid or short-sighted or for being idiotically inconsiderate or selfish. An a——— has a serious character flaw, it usually being that he or she doesn't realize that he or she is an a———.

The *a*-word has become Woofton's, and I dare say America's, favorite cuss-out epithet. The word *ass* used to be heard applied to any special fool. A tame enough epithet. But the second syllable now tacked onto it gives it a pungent anatomical reference that too many people have found increasingly irresistible over the past thirty years. Bless you if you're an exception. But how many members of your family, from eight to sixty, have not used it referentially and irreverently about somebody, or maybe as a parting shot out the window in exasperating traffic encounters? It does the job and seems in no danger of retirement. The *a*-word may be the first two-syllable swear word that Americans find as satisfying as the traditional one-syllable ones. Uttering it—it must be admitted—can have its satisfactions.

Obscene language will, gosh knows, never go away, because it is emotionally so relieving or satisfying in those moments of stress, frustration, or outrage. Human beings occasionally need to blurt, and it's that raw or forbidden expression, the word of one syllable, that readily answers that need. Certainly not all people are for swearing. They're four-square forswearers. They manage to go through life without resorting to nasty speech. But this is less and less true nowadays, when movies, television, radio, and books are riper than they've ever been with four-letter words, to say nothing of popular music lyrics. Even with strict clean-tongued parents, it's difficult for young people to escape the influence of the mass media and its increasingly permissive speech (political correctness notwithstanding).

Scatology is the word usually heard for obscene language, though it chiefly connotes wording having an excremental theme. Two other terms for filthy talk (or presumably the equivalent in writing or print) are *borborology* and *coprolalia*. More interesting, the old words *lalochezia* and *catarolysis* are defined as "filthy talk to relieve tension." Then there's *tapinosis*, not a beer drinker's disease but the use of scurrilous inanimate epithets, such as *scab* or *dumbbell*. You may have encountered the word *logorrhea* for unstoppable blathering or running off at the mouth. Some people, regrettably, not only run off at the mouth but do it mostly with dirty words. We could use another word, *borborrhea* or *coprorrhea*. A four-letter word (which of course need not have four letters), or the use of four-letter words, is sometimes facetiously called a *quadriliteralism*.

Today the art of insult or name-calling seems pretty artless. A possible exception is the world of the military, where it is the training language of boot camp. Back in the Renaissance, Scottish poets made an art out of invective in verse, a genre called *flyting*. African-Americans have the *dozens* (or the *dirty dozens*) or so-called *signifying*, an insult game in which relatives are fair game.

But there generally isn't much wit out there. Most verbal abuse nowadays is unimaginative and repetitious. Unrepeatable words have become all too repeatable. Using those same old taboo words lets off steam but rarely anything freshly cutting or zingerish. Even the term *taboo word* sounds old-fashioned in the 1990s.

When classic taboo words become overused, when one-time barnyard epithets become schoolyard—grammar schoolyard—epithets, are the words really taboo anymore? Nor can we innoculate young people against this.

Epithets are what we use when we abuse others verbally. (As bad as apathetic times are epithetic times, when people resort to characterizing, demonizing, and polarizing name-calling.) An epithet can denote a name or nickname, or it can denote a random curse. The eleven prime profanities I did not spell out above are both senses in one.

We characterize others negatively all the time. So-and-so is a procrastinator. Or so-and-so is variously a *liar, phony, pompous ass, opportunist, operator, hypocrite, maniac, coward, fanatic, cold fish, bore, sicko, know-it-all, bossy person, workaholic, dirty old man, slut, bimbo, windbag, pest.* . . . We get more all-purpose use out of the four-letter thumbs-downers *jerk, nerd, wimp, dork,* and *putz,* to which one could add *schmuck.*

The *a*-word is doubtless here to stay as a name-calling weapon, but wouldn't a less vulgar alternative be nice now and then?

What ever happened to the old-fashioned, non-X-rated *jerk, sap, dumbbell, nitwit, imbecile*? What about *dunce, dolt, buffoon, dingdong, lamebrain, numskull*? English also has a long tradition of all kinds of *-heady* insults, such as *blockhead, puddinghead, bonehead, chowderhead, pinhead, fathead, lunkhead, cabbagehead, pumpkinhead, bubblehead, jughead,* and *knucklehead.*

Blithering idiot used to be a popular insult. *Egregious ass* can give satisfaction, and so can *horse's ass* and—so satisfying—*perfect jackass. Ignoramus* has a good ring to it, and there's no reason why a contemptibly thoughtless person can't be a *selfish ignoramus,* an *utter ignoramus,* or a *breathtaking ignoramus.*

Notice how a pairing of terms, an adjective with a noun, can sound more effective than a single word? This has always been true in the art of insult: You don't just call somebody a blank, you call him or her a blankety-blank.

Enough of this vulgar and tiresome *a*-word, or at least reserve it for special out-of-control occasions. It's plenty possible in our great English language to be properly offensive without being improperly offensive. To this end, here in two columns are a variety of derogatory synonyms for the *a*-word along with a variety of adjectives they can be paired with. In other words, choose any modifier in Column A to combine with any epithet in Column B:

Column A	Column B
real	birdbrain
first-class	numskull
genuine	peabrain
stupid	rattlebrain
blithering	ignoramus
flaming	dingbat
royal	knucklehead
freaking	pinhead
raving	stoopnagel
utter	nitwit
breathtaking	cretin
certifiable	defective
driveling	jackass
out-and-out	lunatic
unmitigated	dumbbell
egregious	nitwit
surpassing	moron
howling	peabrain
king-size	dolt
colossal	jerk
superior	dingdong
vacuous	imbecile
drooling	idiot
arrant	lamebrain
major	nincompoop

prize-winning   doofus
incredible   baboon
unimaginable   dipstick
world-class   ass (holeless)

Remember, while we all have occasion to lose our temper, we need not always loose our worst language. Vulgarity, besides being other things, is almost always overstatement. Try a little understatement. It's less predictable, and it does the job with a touch of class.

The deliberately misspelled word in last week's column was *chifferobe*. It's *chifforobe*.

Nym-'n'-Nyms

WORD OF THE WEEK: *Addisonian termination*—ending a sentence with a preposition

QUOTE OF THE WEEK: "Writing is like walking in a deserted street. Out of the dust in the street you make a mud pie."

—JOHN LE CARRÉ

When a well-meaning and seemingly educated woman recently asked me if a homonym was some kind of troll or munchkin in a homosexual fairy tale, I realized it might be time to say something about a group of somewhat technical but nonetheless useful words—useful because they denote types of words.

Let's call them nym-'n'-nyms.

A *homonym,* of course or not so of course, is a word having both the same spelling and the same sound as another word—for example, *bow* (of a ship), being a homonym of *bow* (to bend over). You're more familiar with *synonym,* referring to a word having the same meaning as another; and its counterpart for a word of opposite meaning, *antonym.* A synonym is like a lost twin in that we're so often searching for one, and we usually find it inside a thesaurus. Not all words have synonyms, but *synonym* has two old ones that are no longer used, *poecilonym* and *polyonym.* A synonym that is euphonious, or pleasing to the ear or mind's ear, is a *euphonym.* And the subject of an earlier Wordwizard column was *retronyms,* newfangled words coined to take back some lost ground in meaning.

What *homonym, synonym,* and *antonym* have in common is that tail end. The suffix *-onym* in English, from Greek, means "word" or "name." The related adjective *onymous* means "bearing a name or a signature" (as that of an author), and *onymatic* means "pertaining to nomenclature."

Any language worth its salt should be able to designate or describe not only the general phenomena of life and the world but also itself—terminology useful for analyzing a language is called a metalanguage. Just as words are indispensable, words for or about words can be useful for anybody, scholar or everyman, who steps back to consider the nuts and bolts of speech itself.

How do we refer to types of words?

One way is through grammatical terminology or names of the parts of speech: noun, pronoun, adjective, adverb, verb, conjunction, preposition, interjection, article. We can talk about common nouns as opposed to proper nouns or active verbs as opposed to passive verbs. Outside of grammar, we have such terms as *blend word* (or *portmanteau word),* *weasel word,* and *loaded word.* There are many *-ism* words, from *Africanism* to *euphemism* to *Yiddishism.*

And there are nym-'n'-nyms, as I call them, words ending in *-onym* that signal specific reference to words that are serving as names. That is, a nym-'n'-nym is a term for a term; a word ending in *-onym* is one coined for scientific or technical use or for indicating a type of name. There are more nym-'n'-nyms in the dictionary than you'd think. Many are rarified and little known but interesting as evidence of the richness of the English language's metalanguage, its vocabulary for discussing itself.

Can you name (not to make a pun) three other *-onym* words besides *homonym, synonym,* and *antonym?*

Onym itself is a word, sans hyphen, and is a good place to start in naming the different naming-words of our language. An onym is simply a technical name, and not surprisingly several *-onym* derivatives are classificational terms of science. An *organonym* is the medical name for an organ of the body. A *hyponym* is a proposed taxonomic term in botany or zoology that is invalid because there is insufficient information about the group being designated. A hyponym is more commonly called a *nomen nudum*, which looks naughtier than it is; and in linguistics a hyponym refers to a subcategory of words, e.g., *sofa* being a hyponym of *furniture*. A *typonym* is a classifying "type" name rather than one devised on a specimen description. A *tautonym* is a double or binomial name for a creature, such as *hush-hush, tom-tom,* or *Mephitis mephitis* for a genus-species of skunk. A *caconym* is an unacceptable taxonomic name.

Of more interest are some fifteen or so other nym-'n'-nyms. You may have encountered *patronym* (or *patronymic*), meaning any name derived from a father or member of the paternal side of the family. Appropriately, there's also *matronym* (and *matronymic*) for a mother-derived name. If need be, there's also *paedonym* (or *tecnonym*) for a child-inspired appellation.

You're probably not familiar with a little-heard counterpart to *homonym: heteronym,* denoting a word having the same spelling as another but not the same pronunciation; *bass* (the fish) and *bass* (the musical instrument) would be heteronyms. What does one call a word in English equivalent or very similar to one in a foreign language, as in the case of *ear* and the German word *Ohr*? A cognate—or a *paronym*.

Words sometimes come from people's names, and an *eponym* is the term for the person from whom a name or word is derived, like *Atlas (atlas), Lesbos (lesbian),* and *Pasteur (pasteurization)*. Other eponymous derivations are *quisling, aphrodisiac, philistine, pompadour, Mae West* (life jacket), *beef Stroganoff,* and *Stetson*. But the word is more and more used to mean the reverse, or the derived name. If we continue to use *eponym* in the latter sense, we'll need another word for its first or name-giving meaning—and we have an old one: *protonym*. A place name, meanwhile, no matter who or what it comes from, is a *toponym*. Not to confuse you, but it then turns out that *Leningrad* (from *Lenin*) can be called both an eponym and a toponym. A foreign version of a place name, such as English *Florence* for Italy's *Firenze,* is an *exonym*.

In the writing life, a false name used by an author is a *pseudonym,* also known as an *anonym*. One's own real name is an *autonym,* which can also refer to a book written under that name. If a writer chooses to be known by his own name spelled backward, he or she is using an *ananym*—not to be confused with *anonym*. By using the name of another person as a pen name, the writer uses an *allonym*. A secret name, guarded by an author or nonauthor, is a *cryptonym*. And what about those aptly named characters inside books, those names we encounter so often in the works of Spenser, Bunyan, and Dickens, in literature from the Bible to Restoration drama, that describe or symbolize the life's role or personal qualities (or lack thereof) of the fictional person: Mr. Worldlywiseman, Mrs. Malaprop, Dr. Dryasdust. They are *aptronyms* (also known as *label names),* a term coined by columnist Franklin P. Adams. The dictionary tells us that the study of personal names is *anthroponymy,* but it doesn't give us the word *anthroponym*.

We can call any term consisting of one word a *mononym*. A particularly exotic nym-'n'-nym is *achthronym,* a word H. L. Mencken used for an ethnic slur (or ethnophaulism).

Finally, our most significant nym-'n'-nym today is the one that saves us words, and often boring institutional words, but that is more prevalent than most of us would like. It takes the initial letter or letters of words in a compound or multiword name and makes them handily into one artificial word, from NATO to NIMBY: the *acronym,* or initialism pronounceable as a word. If we weren't so bureaucratic or impatient in this modern age, maybe we wouldn't need acronyms.

The main thing? Any term or name should be suitable, fitting, appropriate. It should be, as it's termed, a *euonym*.

The deliberately misspelled word in last week's column was *innoculate*. It's *inoculate*.

NOMENCLATURALLY DISADVANTAGED

WORD OF THE WEEK: *chop-logic*—false, tricky, or illogical argumentation

QUOTE OF THE WEEK: "Slovenly language corrodes the mind."

—JAMES TRUSLOW ADAMS

Are you one of the nomenclaturally disadvantaged? Social factionism is abroad (domestically, that is) in the United States as never before, and it's definitely having an effect on the English we use.

It seems a lot of people would much rather be affiliated with a minority group than with a majority group, or with a special-interest group than with an everybody's-interest group. (What ever happened to the commonweal?) Why? A need to feel noticed and respected seems to be a chief reason, and even in Woofton many people, instead of becoming rugged individualists, are choosing to become dogged groupers (not to be confused with groupies).

Self-esteem is very big these days—or it is very small? Day-to-day social intercourse is more and more a delicate matter. Egos are trigger-happy. People are not only sentient (perceptionally aware and responsive), sensate (apprehending through the five senses), and sensitive (emotionally susceptible or edgy). They're downright sensitized (made hypersensitive).

Time was when talk of being sensitive applied mostly to close personal relationships, as when a parent would whisper that her youngest daughter was at a sensitive age. Now beings of all ages can be vociferously sensitive about the way they are treated or addressed or referred to by a passing driver. We're talking not just self-image here. We're talking the English language.

Certainly the United States has been a land of boldly colorful and slangy speech as well as of enduring Puritanism. But if euphemism isn't as American as apple pie, it's at least a force that periodically creeps into our national cultural diet. In the nineteenth century many Americans cultivated a sensitivity about "indelicate" matters and considered much of Shakespeare's language obscene, almost sacrilegious. A lady's leg was preferably a *limb,* and even a chicken leg was a *joint.* Other preferred terms were *lewdness* for *fornication, male cow* for *bull, blood poison* for *syphilis, jackass* for *ass, fallen woman* for *whore,* and *bosom* for *breast* or *breasts.* In our century there have been other "stylings" of everyday language according to the dictates (or dictators) of propriety, including a Hollywood Production Code censoring certain terms in movie scripts.

So benign-izing terminology has something of a tradition in our country. In the case of so-called political correctness, the focus happens to be on sociological sensitivities rather than on sexual taboos or moral or religious standards.

English, like any other language, can blow both ways. One's choice of wording can be positive, or it can be negative. Even facetiously or with a wink, we'll always now and then resort to self-consciously benign phrasings and epithets. One's wife is *my better half,* one's husband *the man of the house* (no longer necessarily *the breadwinner),* one's child *my pride and joy.*

Euphemisms are what we call substitute expressions for that which is thought to be taboo, offensive, or just unpleasant, from sexual matters *(they had relations)* to drunkenness *(had a little too much, is a bit unsteady)* to death (passed away, gone on to a better place). Euphemisms are verbal restoratives. They put things in a good light. At their best, their intentions are good: to spare others gritty or grody detail or to avoid bruising their feelings. At their worst, euphemisms are used to cover up or dress up nasty truths, as when they're used in political, military, or general bureaucratic jargon. Usually a euphemistic expression is longer than what it's substituting for and hence is a kind of premeditated circumlocution, or speaking around something.

The word euphemism has not one but two antonyms, dysphemism and cacophemism, both denoting a disparaging or harsh expression. If you call your girlfriend your most beautiful girl in the world, you are using a euphemism unless she is Miss Universe. If you call her my old lady, you are using a dysphemism. Or a cacophemism, except that cacophemism often is used where the negative wording is used superstitiously, to ward off bad luck. A related and rare word here is cledonism, the avoiding of unlucky words, or the use of euphemism for superstitious reasons or to avert bad luck. Good examples today of cledonism would be some people's avoidance of the word cancer; or that of a baseball pitcher's teammates of the term no-hitter in the dugout during the game, while all are aware that he is completing a game in which he has allowed no hits. Possibly uttering a feared word and then saying "Knock on wood" would also qualify as cledonism.

But what about euphemism in referring to people?

You're encountered those euphemistic, jargonish job titles, like entrenching engineer for ditchdigger. They are often satirized today, but satirized or not, they are still to be found everywhere in the workplace. They've become especially endemic since the 1960s, when much traditional terminology was deemed demeaning, when workers decided a more impressive title might mean a higher salary—or when employers realized a highfalutin job description might quiet an employee's salary dissatisfaction. Our janitors became custodial engineers and our garbage men *sanitation workers.* "The tendency to engaud lowly vocations with names presumably dignified," H. L. Mencken says in *The American Language,* "goes back to the Revolution, and has been frequently noted by English travelers." Among examples Mencken offers in the 1936 edition of his great work are *canine control officer* for dog catcher, *provisioner* for grocer, *educational adviser* for encyclopedia salesman, *waste material dealer* for junkman, *chief lithographer* for (theater) bill sticker, and *footwear maintenance engineer* for *bootblack.* How far do we go here? Should a person who has fleas be called an *insect companion accommodater*?

Along with the occupational ones, other designations have come along for people who are handicapped or disabled. They are now *differently abled.*

What is called a paradigm—or formulaic language pattern—has been created here. As a language-watcher, you should take note of the difference in these usually two-word sensitized (if not sanitized) terms: They have a passive or deterministic connotation, with the final word being not a noun but a participle. This *blank -ed* paradigm has become popular, even contagious.

Obviously, there's a good point to revising language so that unfortunate human beings aren't labeled negatively and stigmatized. (An exception here is the organization Alcoholics Anonymous, whose members often call themselves not alcohol dependent but, plainly, drunks.) Similarly, it is perhaps more useful to call somebody emotionally disturbed than crazy.

But the genuinely afflicted have become only a small part of a drive for recognition and "empowerment" by all manner of people.

Justice-seeking has become very attention-getting.

In what sometimes seems like a mass identity crisis, great numbers of Americans now want to be sociologically euphemized, dubbed according to the *blank -ed paradigm.* Call these participled designations solicitous sobriquets. Call them self-esteemisms. Call them approbationisms. Call them affirmationatives.

Or call them rubadubisms. They dub, and they do it in a rubbing or stroking way; and the word *rub-a-dub* (the *Random House Dictionary* tells us) denotes the sound of a drumbeat—in this case for a minority-rights cause or movement.

In recent years it seems that anybody with any kind of shortcoming or negotiable dissatisfaction has acquired some kind of official rubadubism. Are we indeed becoming—linguistically, at least—a nation of self-styled victims?

Doonesbury creator Garry Trudeau began his 1991 commencement address at Yale University thus: "Dean Kagan, Distinguished Faculty, Parents, Friends, Graduating Seniors, Secret Service Agents, Class Agents, People of Class, People of Color, Colorful People, People of Height, The Vertically Constrained, People of Hair, The Differently Coiffed, The Optically Challenged, The Temporarily Sighted, The Insightful, The Out of Sight, The Out of Towners, The Eurocentrics, The Afrocentrics, Afrocentrics with Eurorail Passes, The Eccentrically Inclined, The Sexually Disinclined, People of Sex, Sexy People, Sexist Pigs, Animal Companions, Friends of the Earth, Friends of the Boss, The Temporarily Employed, The Differently Employed, The Differently Optioned, People With Options, People With Stock Options, The Divestiturists, The Deconstructionists, The Home Constructionists, The Homeboys, The Homeless, The Temporarily Housed at Home, and, God save us, The Permanently Housed at Home:

"In the spirit of the new plurality, I thought I'd begin today by trying to offend all of you all at once, in lieu of my usual practice of offending small, informal groups as I go along. If I have inadvertently left anyone out, I naturally apologize for my insensitivity."

"Our concern for the genuine victims of misfortune or injustice," William Sykes says in A *Nation of Victims,* "is sorely tested as the list of certifiable victims continues to grow; victim status is now claimed not only by members of minority groups but increasingly by the

middle class, millionaire artists, students at Ivy League
colleges, 'adult children,' the obese, codependents, victims of 'lookism' (bias against the unattractive), 'age-
ism,' 'toxic parents,' and the otherwise psychically
scarred—all of whom are now engaged in an elaborate
game of victim one-upmanship. . . . Everybody wants
in on this." Mr. Sykes observes that the politics of vic-
timization has taken the place of more traditional expressions of morality and equity. He mentions the case
of a man with a very large posterior, as opposed to a
very large following, filing an equal-protection com-
plaint against McDonald's because of the small seats in
their restaurants. Possibly the man needed a larger following and a good term for his disadvantaged category.
The seatfully overlapping? The backside-gifted?

Rubadubisms have gone just a little too far—or not
far enough. If there are buffered titles for some people
with problems, why not for all people who are coping in
some way?

What of neglected or malcontented groups who are
not yet the euphemistically acknowledged? What of
those of us for whom the sociopolitical jargonauts have
insensitively neglected to find perfectly unfrank designations? Have those rubadubism-coiners been discriminat-
ingly discriminatory, terminologically elitist?

What of the nomenclaturally disadvantaged?

It's time to lighten up. In the spirit of equal opportunity, Mr. Wordwizard offers the following rubadubisms:

human beings: the species advantaged
huge people: the corporally doubled
chronic criminals (repeat offenders): the recidivism
    abled
ex-cons: the formerly involuntarily secured
chronically late people: the punctuality challenged
school dropouts: the scholastically deferred
people with incomprehensible accents: the inflection
    afflicted
funny-looking people: the differently ogled

bigamists: the matrimonially diversified
rebellious people: the socially combustible
sick (infectious) people: the pathogen cultured
people with drooping flesh: the feature engulfed
adolescents: the hormone dominated
bar pickups: the randomly actionable
false teeth wearers: the plate indentured
bisexuals: the erotically gender-inclusive
people with illegible handwriting: the graphologically
    distressed
looters: the opportunistically merchandise-laden
bald people: the cranially denuded
poor people: the materially chagrined
small-nosed people: the nasally snubbed
jilted people: the romantically supplanted
morning grouches: the matutinally implacable
bad role models: the regrettably exemplary
people who talk out of both sides of their mouth: the
    semantically bilingual
boring people: the charisma unencumbered
clumsy people: the pratfall proficient
stupid people: the cerebrally unabsorbent
easy women: the phallocentrically exploited
impotent men: the briefly upstanding
politically correct people: the willingly offended
not politically correct people: the shibboleth bullied
people who speak in politically correct jargon: the dic-
    tion tortured

If you're nomenclaturally disadvantaged and your
particular identity of choice is not covered here, be creative. You have, above, your paradigm cut out for you.

The deliberately misspelled word in last week's column was *rarified*. It's *rarefied*.

Hyper to Be Correct

WORD OF THE WEEK: *lethologica*—word memory block; tip-of-the-tongueness

QUOTE OF THE WEEK: "Proper words in proper places, make the true definition of a style."

—JONATHAN SWIFT

"He is the one whom I believe lives just outside Woofton."

Can a person ever be too correct grammatically or pronunciationally? The answer is yes, one can be hyper—hypercorrect.

A *hypercorrection* is a form, usage, or pronunciation that is strained and usually erroneous; strained because the perpetrator is holding his or her breath (linguistically) to avoid a supposed error, is ill-advisedly going by analogy with a different expression, or simply has a firmly mistaken notion about the use or meaning of a word.

The person who wrongly uses *whom* when it should be the easier *who* (or vice versa), as in the example sentence above, is hauling a hypercorrection; it is *who* because the pronoun operates as the subject of *lives just outside of Woofton*, not as the direct object of *believe*.

To take another example, one who pronounces—much less spells—*mischievous* "mis-chee-vee-us" is uttering a grievous hypercorrection.

A hypercorrectionist is also one who constantly says *between you and I,* when the (object of a preposition) pronoun should be *me.*

One who repeatedly says *one,* refusing to use *I* or *you* or other nouns or pronouns, is being correct to a hyper and pretentious degree. Such a one is guilty not only of hypercorrection but of *illeism,* the affected use of the third-person pronoun.

If any of these are expressions you sometimes use, it's time you became aware of the foolishness of strained pseudo-correctness. And of the word *hypercorrection.* We have many terms for subgrammatical miscues in English, and it's useful to have one for a symptom of verbal overachieving. (You'll find little or nothing about hypercorrection in usage or grammar books, which prefer to talk about more obvious errors.) Of course, to recognize the phenomenon, it helps to brush up a bit on your grammar and check the dictionary for correct—not hypercorrect—pronunciations once in a while.

What's really unfortunate about any given instance of hypercorrection is not that it's a mistake—we all make verbal mistakes—but rather that it usually betrays a misguided attempt to sound good, at best, and a misguided attempt at airs, at worst.

It's between him and I.
The award was given to him and to myself.
I feel badly.
Oftentimes . . .

What we have here, then, are overcompensations by the grammatically insecure. Many of these overcompensations are fundamentally a kind of aversion behavior—misguided avoiding of other locutions that the speaker feels uncomfortably unsure about or erroneously thinks to be erroneous. Thus you hear somebody saying . . . *to we teachers* . . . (thinking that *to us teachers* sounds vulgar or egotistic); or . . . *don't care whom is at the bottom of this* . . . (showing off an impressive but mistaken use of *whom); or . . . a silvery lake, somewhat as a mirror . . .* (fear of using the word *like* because of some sense of its controversial use as a conjunction, even when it is the correct word); or *tested positively for the virus* (instead of just *positive,* out of the notion that all adverbs should end in *-ly* to be correct); or . . . *left it where it was lying . . .* (instead of using *lay,* the word that everybody is afraid of misusing for *lie).*

It's quite possible that no English expression has inspired so many hypercorrect phrasings as the correct but ever-stilted-sounding *It is I.*

Hypercorrections, then, can be due to plain ignorance or unplain phonyness. At one end of the spectrum you have poorly educated people trying their best to speak well—a kind of linguistic shabby-genteelism. Their *Schlimmverbesserungen* (what the Germans call miscorrections) are at least well meant. Or is it well-ly meant?

At the other end you have utter affectation: an otherwise earthy athlete or entertainer trying to sound but-seriously profound in an interview, or an educationist who knows more pretentious jargon than basic grammar, or a society lady being too-too, or a pedant who loves to be correct but goes wrong from overkill. Whichever the case, incorrect hypercorrections are a bit like pinkies self-consciously waggling when one is lifting a Wedgewood teacup.

A special kind of hypercorrection is the *hyperurbanism,* a rarer term for a dubious usage or pronunciation by someone who wants not to sound countrified or provincial or who tries hard not to reveal that he or she speaks in a dialect that has no prestige. When the insecure farm wife says something like "An' whom might you be?" or pronounces a word a little too carefully, she is growing a hyperurbanism out of season.

What do you call the pronunciations we hear or commit that are carefully syllabic, saying a word syllable by syllable rather than in the natural, fluent way that is favored in the dictionary? For example, pronouncing *carefully* "care-ful-ly" rather than "care-flee," or *sarsaparilla* "sar-sa-par-il-la" rather than "sass-par-il-la"?

You call it a *spelling pronunciation,* and it's a kind of hypercorrection. It's a pronunciation that endures not so much because of continual usage as because of the way readers—or schoolteachers—fancy the word should be pronounced, say, "Green-wich" rather than "Gren-ich" or "sof-o-more" rather than "sof-more." It arises when less sophisticated (or less dictionary-savvy) people attempt to use in speech a word they've seen in print but scarcely heard (these are sometimes called eye words); and when they "figure out" how it should sound, maybe because of its similarity to another word. They go wrong because English is not, never was, and never shall be nicely logical.

In the same vein as the hypercorrection is the *genteelism,* a word favored over another word out of some notion that it is more genteel or classy, such as *abdomen* rather than *belly* or *utensil* rather than *tool.* Genteelisms are not errors, merely synonyms with airs (and are sometimes borderline euphemisms). They may be longer Latinate words rather than simple words, or French borrowings, or archaic words. Obviously there is nothing wrong with a word in itself. All is context or intent, and you can spot a genteelism when it is out of place coming from a certain mouth or when it is just a conspicuously phony choice of wording. Like the *hypocorism,* or pet name, it's often an ineffective affectation.

As for hypercorrect phrases, you'd do well to watch your language and avoid them. To those in the know, they're a giveaway for a brave but inadequate education in English, no matter how rich or well-dressed or nice a person the speaker is.

The deliberately misspelled word in last week's column was *sacreligious.* It's *sacrilegious.*

WORD AUTHORS

WORD OF THE WEEK: *antonomasia*—using an epithet or nickname for somebody

QUOTE OF THE WEEK: "No passion in the world is equal to the passion to alter someone else's draft."

—H. G. WELLS

What do these words have in common: *relationship, blurb, centrifugal, cafeteria,* and *braintrust*? Your clue is "origins."

The common thread here is that we know that each was coined—or, in some cases, popularized and really put into general circulation—by a particular individual: *relationship* by the English poet Alexander Pope, *blurb* by the American humorist Gelett Burgess, *centrifugal* by the English physicist Isaac Newton, *cafeteria* by the American entrepreneur John Kruger, and *braintrust* by the American reporter John Kieran.

But these are rare detections. Have you ever stopped to think that the great preponderance of words in English—or in any other language—are author-unknown words?

As hard as it may be to utter or write something that will become a famous line to be remembered and quoted, it's *much* harder to invent or promote a single word that will get used everywhere and pass into the language (and that you can mention on your resumé).

To concoct one is easy enough. There have been many, usually humorous articles and books proposing new words over the years. But to concoct a word that ends up in the dictionary—in a word, it's a long shot.

Inventors (or designers) of large vehicles, small gadgets, formulas, and disease cures usually get patents and credit. Why not inventors of words?

The knack for cleverness in coining words is called *logodaedaly,* but that covers only the making up of them, not their successful distribution and longevity. And even when a word is traceable to one person, how many people are aware who coined it? (Test this yourself with the words below.)

How many wordwrights can you name? No, there's no such word as *wordwright,* but why not try it out here?

Among those who have made single-word contributions to the English language are John Milton *(earthshaking, impassive, lovelorn, pandemonium, sensuous),* Robert Browning *(artistry),* Lewis Carroll *(galumphing, chortle),* Sir Thomas Browne *(electricity),* Lord Byron *(blasé),* H. L. Mencken *(booboisie* and *ecdysiast,* for stripteaser), Edmund Burke *(diplomacy),* Samuel Taylor Coleridge *(intensify),* Thomas Carlyle *(self-help),* Thomas Jefferson *(belittle),* Oliver Wendell Holmes *(anesthesia),* and Sir Walter Scott *(blackmail, gruesome).* At least, they were the first to use these in print, and that's the usual criterion for wordwright credit. Terms can also be two or more words, of course. *Runcible spoon* was coined by Edward Lear and *Bermuda Triangle* by Vincent Gaddis, a writer. Teddy Roosevelt is given credit for *lunatic fringe, pussyfoot,* and *mollycoddle.* Known logodaedalists all.

Neologisms are what we call new words, fresh out of the mouths not of babes but of adults. A neologism is new, but it may last, whereas an original makeshift term for a particular occasion or piece of writing is called a *nonce word.* The nonce word is instant and unlasting. Or is it? Many, so labeled, can be found in the big unabridged dictionaries, but they lie forgotten.

People have been contributing their self-devised words to English for centuries. When there's no existing word for something, why not fill the need? Aware of the strong Latin and Greek underpinnings in our language, many coiners combine Latin and Greek elements to forge new words. But they don't always catch on. Many ripely pedantic Latinisms were ventured (some with tongue in cheek) by writers living at the height of the Renaissance. Many passed into the language, but quite a few were short-lived—for example, *obtestate,* "to beseech." Today they're called *inkhorn words* or *inkhornisms.*

Maybe everybody has a word he or she wants to get in (to the dictionary) edgewise. "An astonishing number of people believe that new words are invented by individuals, and in an effort to be helpful they devise a list of neologisms of their own, which they kindly make available for inclusion in the next edition of one's dictionary," lexicographer Sidney Landau relates in his fine book on dictionary-making. "Some correspondents are quite proud of the new words they have devised and feel that the dictionary editor owes them a debt of gratitude. I have received letters from correspondents who offered to sell me their neologisms at ten dollars each and were aggrieved when I declined to purchase them."

Over the centuries many attempts to coin words (if not for personal credit) have failed. You may have seen a number of recent "words we could really use" books that have been published, but it seems that the words we could really use almost never become the words we really do use. Humorist Gelett Burgess (1866–1951), who succeeded with *blurb* and *bromide,* offered America a whole glossary of Burgessisms that are now only a historical curiosity. Among his neologisms in *Burgess Unabridged: A New Dictionary of Words You Have Always Needed* (1914) are *cowcat,* "a person whose main function is to occupy space"; *gixlety,* "brutal kindness" or "misguided hospitality"; and *spillix,* "undeserved good luck."

Many words, of course, are intentionally strange or humorous—you've probably made up a few yourself to use with your family or share with your friends (see Paul Dixon's book *Family Words*). In our country outlandish mock-Latin words of more than one syllable *(plurisyllables)* go back to the frontier days of colorful boasting and tall tales. Even single words were windy, such as (all author unknown) *rambunctious* ("uncontrollable"), *absquatulate* ("to leave in a stealthy way"), *ramsquaddle* ("to beat"), *callithumpian* ("a noisy parade"), and *conbobberation* ("disturbance"). In the nineteenth century the young but healthy American language also came up with (unsigned) *shebang, skedaddle, sockdolager, shindig, splendiferous,* and *slumgullion.* (What is it about words beginning with *s?*) Children's stories have also given the adult world a few lasting words. To mention two, there's *supercalifragilisticexpialidocius* from *Mary Poppins* and *grinch* from Dr. Seuss's *The Grinch Who Stole Christmas.* Above all, there is Lewis Carroll's *Alice's Adventures in Wonderland,* which has given us *jabberwocky* and *Humpty-Dumpty* (a character name, admittedly, but a word too; today we call a word that seems to be used to mean anything a *Humpty-Dumpty word*).

Then there are words that don't really exist but by some mistake—a scribe working under deadline pressure, perhaps—make it into the dictionary. A famous example arose when a lexicographer noted *"D. or d."* next to the scientific abbreviation for "density." Lo, the false word *dord,* for "density," showed up in the pages of a large dictionary *(Merriam-Webster's Second International).* It's called a *ghost word.* Not so much coined as misbegotten, and nobody knows its author, fortunately for him or her.

Sometimes who the actual coiner of a vocable (a vocable is more or less a word considered apart from its meaning) is can't be proven, but who popularized the word is known for sure. Such is the case with *weasel word* and *lunatic fringe,* both popularized by Teddy Roosevelt. If a word-popularizer is less a coiner than a distributor, he or she can be just as important in (no apologies for the pun) getting the word out.

Besides Shakespeare, who was the conjurer not only of our greatest plays but also of the words *critic, livery, auspicious, aerial,* and *assassination,* two Americans deserve mention.

One is none other than Mark Twain, who gave us, besides America's most beloved novel, *Huckleberry Finn,* the terms *ex-convict, barbed wire, cussword, dust storm, hayride, race prejudice,* and *Wild West.*

The other great American wordwright was Tad. Tad who? Just Tad, or Thomas Aloysius Dorgan, a popular cartoonist at the turn of the century. Tad introduced Americans to *drugstore cowboy, yes-man, lounge lizard, the once-over, hot dog,* and *applesauce* (meaning "phony flattery"). According to H. L. Mencken, the word *hard-boiled* first appeared in one of Mark Twain's speeches but was really popularized by Tad.

Curiously, American cartoonists seem to have had some magic touch (or the best exposure) for word-coining. Another cartoonist named Billy De Beck gave us *heebie-jeebies, hotsy-totsy, hot mama,* and *horse feathers,* and Elzie Crisler Segar, who created *Popeye,* popularized *hamburger* through his character Wimpy (no connection with the word *wimp* today).

Many more words coined or popularized by known wordwrights can be found in H. L. Mencken's wonderful book, *The American Language.* Among them are *yellow dog* (Abraham Lincoln), *normalcy* (Warren Harding), *off the record* (Al Smith), *dust bowl* (Edward Stanley), *sundae* (George Giffy), *scofflaw* and *whoopee* (Henry Irving Shaw), *phooey* (Walter Winchell), *self-determination* (Woodrow Wilson), *agnostic* (Aldous Huxley), *atoll* (Charles Darwin), *motorcade* (Lyle Abbott), *sloganeer* (Richard Connell), *McCarthyism* (Max Lerner), *debunk* (William E. Woodward), *sanitize* (Leon Henderson), and *to jell* (Louis—not Louisa—M. Alcott).

Even a few well-known brand names are credited to enterprising individuals, among them *Kodak* (George

Eastman), *Vaseline* (Robert A. Chesebrough), *Kelvinator* (Major Nathaniel B. Wales), *Kewpie* (Rose Cecil O'Neill Wilson), and *Coca-Cola* (J. S. Pemberton, an Atlanta druggist). More generically, *typewriter* was coined by one Christopher Latham Sholes.

And you? Possibly you'd fancy becoming a word-wright. The trick is, again, not merely the inventing but the getting it into circulation. If you've come up with a new word you think the world is waiting for, you could try just dropping it in conversation, probably having to explain its meaning each time, and crossing the fingers of your writing hand.

But the odds for your word reaching millions will be much better if you (1) write a popular book in which your word figures prominently or repeatedly, (2) get a famous or important personage to use your word, or (3) be in the right situation (a debate with the president?) at the right time (halftime at the Super Bowl?), where your offering will be stunningly and unforgettably public.

The deliberately misspelled word in last week's column was *Wedgewood*. It's *Wedgwood*.

AWKWORDS AS COLLECTIBLES

WORD OF THE WEEK: *orismology*—the science of defining technical terms

QUOTE OF THE WEEK: "Literature is the art of writing something that will be read twice."

—CYRIL CONNOLLY

Anything unusual to you about these two trios of words: (1) *inamissible, jacal,* and *omentum;* and (2) *aviador, maidan,* and *accidity*?

Spelling is a problem for many of us, but even then certain things we see in print jump out at us. Surely those words above in (1) should be *inadmissible, jackal,* and *momentum* because they're missing a letter. And surely the words in (2) are misspellings for *aviator, maiden,* and *acidity*.

Surely not, for all six are legitimate old words found in the pages of the English language's greatest dictionary, the *Oxford English Dictionary* or OED. And they only scratch the surface. How about *allegator, clarety, cingular, pererration, religate . . . ?* The wondrously odd, misspelled-looking collectibles you'll find within the OED and in other large, so-called unabridged dictionaries are virtually numberless.

Words like *adience, bangalow, carotte, deasil, ectatic, fillipeen, gravidate, habnab, illaborate, jerque, kaki, lounderer, mandatary, neumatic, onerary, paeon, qa-*

landar, rabbet, salebrity, tecnology, undigenous, veneficial,
warehous, xeraphim, yirning, Zizyphus. . . .

I call them awkwords.

Why provide you with the meanings of these awkwords when you can have fun looking them up for yourself? (And when we don't have enough space in this column to do that.)

There are so many good reasons for you to browse through the OED, and awkwords—those unfamiliar but legitimate historical English words that look to us like misspellings of words we know—is one of the loonier but quite enjoyable ones. (There is no linguistic term I've been able to uncover for this seeming misspelling "effect.") If some old word is so obscure that it's never seen nor heard, what's it good for?

It's good as a collectible, a bona fide awkword.

. . . *accension, bernicle, chapiter, depravation, elavate,*
forgeful, geep, herem, inermous, juglar, karrusel, loxygen,
maritorious, nithing, orchestia, papulated, quean, ressort,
secretory, telligraph, viraginity, werdrobe . . .

I'm sharing my own personal collection of awkwords with you, not only to lure you into the edifying joys of a *big* dictionary (at our Woofton Library if you don't own one) but because I think awkwords are a fascinating phenomenon.

Think of it. Other words are interesting for their meaning, derivation, pronunciation, or length (sesquipedality, if they're very long), or maybe for being the same word when read backward (palindromic). Awkwords, however, are unique. They just get under your skin visually, to mix a metaphor. An awkword just looks wrong, out of kilter. Inescapably, because it's not (usually) in current general usage, it looks like a word we know that has been jumbled by a sloppy writer or typesetter.

It reminds us how literally spell-bound our reading eyes are.

The awkword's "wrongness" is indeed in the eye of the beholder. It almost disturbs you with its literal (meaning "letter-al") not-quiteness. It hits a button, the reader's reflexive "Ah, obviously *that* is the word that was meant" button. It is a wretched victim of mistaken identity.

. . . *afternan, barbitone, centry, diduction, eagre, frixion, galop, hostelity, insipient, jirble, kokoon, linguished, messuage, nycterine, orignal, prase, quittor, roadeo, sennit, tradevman, volentine, wynd, zibeline* . . .

These old look-alikes also serve to remind us how amazing our English tongue is in its infinite capacity for completely different words that are separate only by a single letter or two or a slight difference in letter order. Our discombobulated reaction to seeing an awkword— or many awkwords—tells us something about our taught or ingrained vocabularies, the usage we're comfortable with.

. . . *adition, barathrum, candys, discide, euphorbia, facund, golilla, housebote, invious, Kuban culture, laager, monogony, ocellate, peepul, regelate, scend, tatou, vigidity, wistaria* . . .

But the best thing about these forgotten rococo words wrongly accused by our modern-English eyes is that when several of them are gathered in a list or a paragraph, the effect is almost physically upsetting to the literate eye. Regarding such a critical mass of seeming cacography (bad spelling) is like being confronted with one of those perception-bending optical riddles or a self-referential riddle drawing by M. C. Escher. It's like seeing a framed picture hanging crookedly on a wall.

. . . *acology, biliteral, cataclasm, deligation, ereption, feracious, groyne, harras, inion, juise, kiack, louvar, matrass, nomic, obrogation, placcate, quacksalver, restaur, secund, torminal, villein, whappet* . . .

By now, with all the awkwords I've cruelly scattered between paragraphs before your eyes, you deserve to know the meaning of a few. Needful to reiterate, virtually all awkwords are rare, technical, archaic, or obsolete terms. You might consider not dropping them in conversation.

Archelogy (as opposed to *archeology*) is the science of first principles. An *aviador* (as opposed to an *aviator*) is a person who supplies money or goods in order to carry on an industry, especially the mining industry. A *chapiter* (as opposed to a *chapter*) is the capital of an architectural column. *Clarety* (as opposed to *clarity*) means "of a variably yellowish dark red color, like that of claret wine." *Deasil* (as opposed to *diesel*) means "right-handwise, sunwise, or clockwise." *Cingular* (as opposed to *singular*) means "pertaining to or shaped like a ring," or annular. *Ectatic* (as opposed to *ecstatic*) means "involving the expansion of a hollow or tubular organ." *Illaborate* (as opposed to *elaborate*) means "rough or carelessly done." *Inamissible* (as opposed to *inadmissible*) means "incapable of being lost." *Regelate* (as opposed to *regulate*) is "to freeze together again"; and to *religate* (as opposed to *relegate*) is "to bind, connect, or bring together." A *tatou* (as opposed to a *tattoo*) is a giant armadillo. *Tecnology* (as opposed to *technology*) is a term for the scientific study of the life and development of children, otherwise known as pedology.

Awkwords are the orthographic bizarreries—or spelling curiosities—of the English language. May your curiosity drive you to those big dictionaries at the public library.

. . . *cryptogam, dorbel, edea, emptional, fantigue, insolation, statice, streeking, suety* . . .

The deliberately misspelled word in last week's column was *resumé*. It's *résumé*, with two acute accents.

HEARD WORDS AND
DECADE DENTS

WORD OF THE WEEK: *antisyzygy*—an oxymoron, or incongruous pairing of terms

QUOTE OF THE WEEK: "No one can write decently who is distrustful of the reader's intelligence, or whose attitude is patronizing."

—E. B. WHITE

The millenium is coming, as a reality instead of as a biblical or apocalytic conception. A few years hence —less than ten, in fact—we will be at the year 2000. It's a good time for some linguistic stock-taking, or word-stock stock-taking. Two questions:

(1) Which individual words would you guess are the most common, or frequently used, in English today?

(2) A decade from now, which will be the words you'll recall as having been the most popular in speech and writing during the 1990s?

Word frequency, as it is called, is difficult to determine by any method or approach, and not surprisingly such investigations have been few and far between over the past century. When they are ventured, linguists can only try to measure frequency in print. From periodicals, newspapers, and books a team of people or, today, a computer can handily scan pages and list and count words.

What kind of words appear most frequently in print? Nouns? Pronouns? Adjectives? Pronouns, yes, but otherwise the words we use the most are those minor words of meaning, the ones that set up or connect the substantive nouns, the main verbs, the coloring and qualifying modifiers: articles, prepositions, conjunctions, auxiliary verbs, and pronouns. In short, what are called particles.

A study more than half a century ago by scholar Edward Thorndike confirmed something else, namely, that most of the frequently used words in English are of native, or Anglo-Saxon, origin rather than being borrowed from (chiefly) Latin, Greek, and French. This despite the fact that, quantitatively, only about one-fifth of the twenty thousand most common words are of Old or Middle English derivation, with some three-fifths of them foreign borrowings. But a few simple, one-syllable homebred words are our conversational workhorses. As one authority has put it, "One-fourth of the task of expression in English is accomplished . . . by just nine words."

The nine words? They are, in descending order of estimated frequency, *and, be, have, it, of, the, to, will,* and *you;* they are followed by *I, a, on, that,* and *is.* (You can remember the nine, although not in their descending order, by memorizing the sentence "And you have the will to be of it.")

An earlier study yielded a slightly different top nine: *the, of, and, to, a, in, that, it,* and *is.* From yet a different study cited by the late polyglot author and professor Mario Pei, the order came out *I, the, and, to, of, in, we, for,* and *you.* A *World Almanac* frequency count made in 1950 gave the top twelve as *the, of, and, a, to, in, is, you, that, it, he,* and *for.*

More recently, we have computer-gathered data on word frequency in print in a single year, 1961, from a study prepared at Brown University. More than a million words of text from all kinds of publications and books were sampled and ranked according to general frequency. The top nine words in this respected, more detailed Brown study do not depart greatly from those listed in the earlier studies, and here are the top twenty-five: *the, of, and, to, a, in, that, is, was, he, for, it, with, as, his, on, be, at, by, I, this, had, not, are,* and *but.*

Stuart Berg Flexner reported in *I Hear America Talking* (1976) that the ten most common words in our country are *I, you, the, a, he, she, it, we, they,* and *me* (with *him, her,* and *them* following).

The front-runners, whatever their order, should not be all that different today or any day. Our English, written or spoken, doesn't change all that much.

What about word frequency in *spoken* English? That's anybody's guess, and I would have said that many words at the top of the list would likely be the same as those in the aforementioned studies.

I said it, and then I spent much of my invaluable free time doing a kind of oral-English field study in Woofton. Which words, I wondered, are you likely to hear the most in stores, restaurants, movie lobbies, telephone conversations?

The words—or sounds—I kept hearing over and over again were a little different. So different that a few of them aren't actual words. I think the modest report I wrote suggests that we don't at all talk the way we write. My little study isn't at all a scholarly one, but it entailed tireless eavesdropping and note-taking. The findings were a little surprising to me, as they may be to local readers who, weeks back, sent in their guesses as to which words would turn out to be the most commonly heard in everyday Woofton conversation.

Adult video was a guess by not one but three people who wrote in—wrong, unfortunately, apart from the fact that it's two words, not one. Among other nominations for the region's most prevalent single uttered word were *homeless, cool, racism, Preparation-H, expensive, mall,* and *ribbed.* None of these made the Voice of the People Top 25. Nor did *Patricia,* submitted by numerous young Woofton males who are acquainted with a young woman employed at a local riding stable.

Here are the twenty words—well, verbalisms—I heard most frequently in conversation around our town:

yunno ("He's kind of weird, yunno?")

dunno ("I dunno, I just dunno.")

um ("Um, I'll get back to you on, um, that.")

yeah ("Yeah, I'd be a good receptionist.")

well ("Yeah, well, okay." "Well, well, look who's
   here.")

uh ("Uh, not exactly.")

huh ("Huh?")

uh-huh ("Uh-huh . . . uh-huh . . . uh . . . huh. . . .
   I've gotta hang up now.")

uh-uh ("Uh-uh, no way.")

what ("What?")

say ("Say, who's in charge here?" "I'll say.")

oh ("Oh." "Oh yeah?" "Oh, no!" "Oh?")

like ("Like, it was, like, like a circus in there.")

sure ("Sure. Absolutely.")

right ("Right . . . right . . .")

okay ("Yeah, well, okay.")

hey ("Hey, could you give me a hand here?" "Hey, I
   wasn't born yesterday.")

yup ("Yup, that's right.")

so ("So?" "So, here we are.")

nah ("Nah. Never.")

So much for word frequency in the here and now.
What about the more high-profile words of the premil-
lennium decade that we're living in now, and how well
they'll be remembered and associated with our decade
less than ten years from now?

How good are you at thinking ahead to thinking back
—at projected retrospection? Can you imagine yourself
ahead to then in order to look back at now?

Historical perspective is always worth cultivating,
even historical perspective regarding language. There's
no better way to inspire your projected retrospection
about the here and now ("projected retrospection" is an
interestingly paradoxical term, not quite an oxymoron)
than to look back on the there and then: in this case, on

recent decades and particular words that became indelibly associated with them.

Like when the word *life-style* (by now *lifestyle,* sans hyphen) became all the rage. Or earlier, when we talked about a person having not a lifestyle but a *complex.* Or later, when we said a lifestyle of complexes was *dysfunctional.*

Times and trends move along so quickly—or faddishly, or impatiently—in the United States of America that it's easy to forget what our conversations sounded like only ten or twenty years ago, and the in-fashion words that made dents in each decade (hence the title above). Our culture, too much of it pop culture, is indeed an impatient one. The working vocabulary of Americans is always moving right along.

But let's throw some perspective on our 1990s by moving back to the 1950s, 1960s, 1970s, and 1980s. We hear about zeitgeists, or cultural, political, and moral "climates" of particular periods. Little zeitgeists often have their own characteristic lingos, and merely eyeing a list of the then–au courant terminology of an age or decade can often give a fair sense of the zeitgeist. In other words, sometimes "ten words or less" *can* sum up the tenor and temper of a time.

What were some of the expressions—the overused ones—that were not necessarily coined during those recent American decades but that are especially associated with those times? What were some of the vogue words, buzz words, pet expressions or our decedent decades?

It'll help if you're more than fifty years old. If you're younger, consider this a brief excursion back through recent verbal history. Americans like to get nostalgic about songs of bygone decades. Why not also about our passing vocabulary hit parade?

Now, designating "decadeisms" is an inexact science. In some cases, whether a term is more associated with one decade than another is quite debatable—particularly when the word has been overused for twenty-five or thirty years. The words singled out here were *not necessarily born* during these ten-year periods. *Cutting edge,* for example, was used metaphorically back in the 1950s, but it's only more recently that its freshness has become tiresomely blunted. The emphasis here is on terms that, to a great extent, made it into mainstream usage.

The 1950s, lying so shyly back there behind the obstreperous 1960s, were flavored by terms from Freud, advertising, the beatniks, some best-selling books *(The Organization Man, The Lonely Crowd, The Hidden Persuaders),* materially comfortable middle-class America, and above all the anxieties of the Cold War and the new nuclear technologies.

Among its memorable words are *complex* (as in *inferiority complex* and *Oedipus complex), conformity* and *conformist* (and their counterparts, *nonconformity* and *nonconformist), conspicuous consumption, phony, crazy, cat, hip* and *hipster, beat* and *beatnik* (and other *-niks,* after *Sputnik), Daddy-O, to bug* (someone), *subliminal, brinkmanship,* and *McCarthyism.* There was television in the 1950s, but the mass media were not so extensive and powerful as they were soon to become. Fewer words and phrases were used to death.

Then came the explosively counter- and anti- 1960s, which had a much bigger mouth, one defiantly anti-intellectual and nongrammatical. Our word-stock met Woodstock. Our language contexts were the civil rights revolution, the Vietnam War and the peace movement, the space race, the Beatles, getting high, three traumatic assassinations in the United States, and ten billion T-shirts and buttons bearing antic slogans. The words of the decade included *militant, organize, groovy, relevant, sit-in, rap* (the nonmusical type), *dialogue* (of the social-political, offstage variety), *credibility gap, far out, freak out, flick, right on, sit-in, where it's at, meaningful, honky, turn on, drop out, psychedelic, tripping, man* (as a form of direct address or hip or hippie sigh), *establishment, counterculture, military-industrial complex, tie-dye, heavy, charisma, value judgment, radicalized,* and *simplistic.*

The country could only take a breath and turn inward in the 1970s, which gave us *Watergate, leisure suits, discos,* and all kinds of getting-in-touch-with-yourself movements and seminars. We heard a lot about *state-of-the-art, viable alternative, finalize, prioritize, stonewalling, ongoing, detente, viable, what's coming down, women's lib* (as women's rights was then so irreverently called), *silent majority, sharing, space* (the personal, not the outer kind), *holistic, centered, touchy-feely, karma* (usually bad), *life-style, self-actualization, swinger, mellow, hunk, getting in touch with one's feelings, bicoastal,* (being) *into* (something), *nonjudgmental, macho, parenting, quality time, bonding,* and *up front.* This was also the decade when the word *major* went into major overuse.

Particularly material or high-rolling capitalist words were far from immaterial in the 1980s, notably *yuppie, trickle-down, the bottom line, the down side, done deal, leveraged* (buyout), *power lunch, across the board, private sector, feeding frenzy, spin doctor, worst-case scenario, interface, across the board, infrastructure, networking, ballpark figure, cutting edge, window of opportunity, baby boomer, cautiously optimistic, sea change.* . . . But let's not forget also *venue, impact, Moral Majority, yo, wannabe, couch potato, community, awesome, Valley girl, chill out, dude, grody, no way, postmodern, sound bite, deconstructed, arguably, at risk, -bashing, in your face, going ballistic, parameter, reality check, on a scale from 1 to 10, community, karaoke, hip-hop, world-class, chill out, community, infotainment, up to speed, on a roll, push the envelope, no pain no gain.* . . . And such social-unhealth jargon as *nurturing, safe sex, dysfunctional, codependent, in denial, twelve-step program, enabler, validate, offensive, supportive, stressed-out, sends the wrong message, wellness, reach out, tough call* . . . to say nothing of *user-friendly* and countless other computer terms.

And here we are, lingually, early in the 1990s and

headlonging toward nothing less than the end of our century and the portentous year 2000.

Is it too early to venture some guesses as to what will be remembered as the terms of this decade?

How about *empowerment, sexual harassment, politically correct, family values, channel surfing, demonize, grunge, wake-up call, this sucker, downsizing,* (not a) *happy camper, to trash* (somebody), *wiggle room, go that extra step, role model, negativity, party animal, ethnic cleansing, no-brainer, entrepreneurial, the healing process, over the top. . . .*

The deliberately misspelled word in last week's column was *rococco.* It's *rococo.*

CONVERSATIONAL CRUTCHES

WORD OF THE WEEK: *Quinalpus*—an authority cited to win an argument

QUOTE OF THE WEEK: "How can I know what I think till I see what I say?"

—E. M. FORSTER

How many Americans today could live without them?

Could the prodigious preponderance (otherwise known as the vast majority) of the citizenry of Woofton, not to say the United States of America, get through a single day without using at least one or two of them?

Let's get personal: Could you?

I'm not talking about cans of diet soda, video movies, or slices of pepperoni pizza.

I'm talking about slices of predictable phraseology, or pet expressions that badly need a leash. In a previous column, my theme was word frequency. But what about whole phrase or sentence incontinence?

The results are in on Mr. Wordwizard's field study to determine the Top Twenty-five Painfully Overused Expressions in Woofton today. I wanted it to be a Top Ten, but there are far too many. In this case, by *expressions* is meant not single words or terms but ready-made comments.

You can run from them, but you can't hide from them.

This crusading column would like to see them at least temporarily banned, if only out of mercy to those of us who inwardly groan at people whose vocabulary runs on automatic pilot. If we can't get bans, we'll settle for— anti-banns? The word with the extra *n* is a public notice of an intended marriage. Let's put these bromides on notice for a full-scale divorce, or at least a temporary separation.

Possibly (before you read further) you'd like to guess some of Woofton's Top Twenty-five Painfully Overused Expressions?

Would one of them be *How are things? See you around? Allow me to introduce . . . ? Thanks very much?*

Not at all. These are useful and certainly still heard, but they're not members of the 1990s verbal virus squad.

I wish I could say that this local investigation of current banalities required my going out into the field far and wide. It did, in the sense that Mr. Wordwizard has spent much of his spare time loitering and listening undercover, pocket pad in hand, at Woofton's major places of public discourse. These include various stores, restaurants, movieplex lobbies, a few school sports events, and our Emporia Shopping Mall. But I scarcely needed to go into the field. The inescapable phrases came right to my door. Unstoppably, they came from the mouths of delivery people, neighbors, and people at the other end of the telephone.

I wish I could say that the utterers apologized for or caught themselves using these thoroughly worn-out and reflexive expressions after the sixth or seventh time within five or ten sentences. But the conversational crutches were spoken quite obliviously and repeatedly. It reminded me of *The Invasion of the Body Snatchers.*

Until recently there were the Unicorn Hunters, a language whistleblower organization founded at Lake Superior State University in 1970–71. Each New Year's

Day the Unicorn Hunters issued a list of words or phrases to be "banished" from the English language "because of mis-use, over-use, or general uselessness." The Unicorn Hunters are no more, but guided by Mr. Thomas Pink of the office of public relations, Lake Superior State University still publishes an annual calendar of words and phrases (nominated by people from all over) that richly deserve exile to the plains of Mars. A most worthy group of watchdogs, in an age when all it takes for an expression to become contagious and empty overnight is a few talk-show, stand-up-comic, or political lingo-slingers and the coast-to-coast power of television.

Among the bromides pilloried by the Unicorn Hunters over the past thirty-some years are *at this point in time* (1976), *you know* (1978 and 1979), *Have a nice day* (1978), and *mandate* (1985).

Notice something depressing about these examples?

Exactly. At least the first three are very much still with us. If modish moronisms flourished only for one year and then vanished—we should be so lucky. They stay around. They stick to the tongues of all of those who utter before they think and who, in fact, feel more comfortable doing things in that order.

Clichés, it's important to emphasize, are *not* bad per se. They are an essential part of any language, and overfamiliar to us though they seem to be, we could not live easily without them. They are ready-made phrasings that, at their best, are immediately understood. They can be very handy as communicational shortcuts. Trying to avoid clichés can often involve you in some tortured wordiness, and for your efforts you may even end up not being understood.

But whole voguish comments or responses, those mindlessly allowed in the front door or the back door of every other bit of conversation, are superclichés. They are locutions that—largely because of the power of mass media today—become reflexes of chat. Overused, they can only become more and more meaningless. They're not one-liners. They're no-brainer one-liners.

What's wrong with relying on stock sentences (or minor sentences) incessantly?

It's unfortunate but true: With a clichéd mouth usually goes a clichéd mind.

A clichéd mind is one satisfied to dress its thoughts in off-the-rack phraseology. If you find yourself parroting trendy flavor-of-the-year expressions recurrently, you probably are happily lost in the limited perspectives and mind-set of the current age and its fashions. Culturally, you're perhaps less a child of your own times than a victim of them. Your mode of thinking is stuck in a nearsightedly contemporary gauge. That is, if you lack a historical perspective, you probably lack a verbal one, too. What's more, trendy expressions are by definition fleeting (at least, most of them are; we will never escape *Have a nice day*). If something is "in," you can bet it'll sooner or later be "out."

English is a wonderfully rich and large language. We should be thankful for it. Rather than mouthing the same borrowed phrasings all the time, why not be a little more individual and original? Forego the obvious. When you can be a verbal plotter, why be a verbal blotter?

Tiresomeness is no crime in English, and we can't make conversational crutches go away. But we can at least—to borrow one that's currently on the used-to-death hit parade—give it a rest.

Here are Mr. Wordwizard's Top Twenty-five Painfully Overused Expressions. (If I added a twenty-sixth, no way it wouldn't be *no way*.) They're in no particular order. Lose them, don't use them.

1. *Tell me about it.* Everybody's now-favorite way of saying "You think this problem impresses me?" or "Believe me, I know just what you mean." Or is it "I've got problems of my own"? It's fast-food sardonicism.

2. *Have a nice day.* I'm sorry, it just won't go away. It's

the password of robotic sincerity. One theory is that it began several decades ago when a woman ordered her son to say something nice to his mean old uncle Ernie, an accused vampire. He could only come up with this.

3. *No problem.* What ever happened to "I'd be glad to," "Not at all," "Don't mention it," or "My pleasure"? They're now too cordial and too corny. Police movies and television shows love this one.

4. *You got it!* Basically an affirming exclamation of phony bonhomie or macho "street" enthusiasm. What does it mean? Who knows, but we've got it.

5. *Give me a break!* The new all-occasion substitute for "You've got to be kidding!" "Come off it!" "You can't be serious!" "Too much!" and other responses that would give us a break from this.

6. *Don't even think about it.* The battle cry of pessimistic or paranoid mind-reading. It's meant to be sort of humorously confrontational.

7. *Can we cut to the chase?* Pseudo-Hollywood talk, and a not unexpected cliché in an age of ever longer video-watching and ever shorter attention spans.

8. *Or something like that.* The Wordwizard theory is that this expression accounts for at least 23 percent of all script lines in television soap operas and movie melodramas. It's supposed to signal cool understatement or hip irony, but it's really fallen archness.

9. *All right!* Or "Awwriiiight!" It used to be "Way to go!" "Good for you!" "Yippee!" "My congratulations!" "Terrific!" or "Great!" This is the latest team-spirit version of enthusiastic approval and is always slurred with false heartiness. Usually a shrug and a "Really?" is all that is genuinely meant.

10. *Or whatever.* This is becoming an all-purpose, can't-be-bothered trailer for standard sloppy or apathetic communication. Judging by the rate that its use—and the mental sloth behind it—is spreading, it may soon be appearing in scholarly theses and academic journals in place of *et cetera* and *et al.*

11. *You don't need to be a rocket scientist* . . . It used to

be *brain surgeon,* but talk shows and ten thousand stand-up comics on television each week have beat this cliché into the American brainpan.

12. *Get a life!* A catchy little exhortation, until it became the favorite (glib and smug) one-liner and throwaway line of half the American population.

13. *You guys . . .* This used to be blue-collar or Hollywood gangster talk. Then it became a standard form of address among all males. Now it's a forced code word of egalitarianism. It's brightly favored, rather self-consciously, by individuals addressing mixed company or by women addressing other women, presumably to reassure them how down-to-earth, gender blind, and casually nonconfrontational they are. It's simple and useful, just a little overused and pretentiously unpretentious. There are rumors of its coming adaptation in Bible translations and liturgies as the modern way to address God.

14. *It sends the wrong message.* This started as the battle cry of "caring" pundits and spokespersons. Now it helps everyone to feel like a caring pundit or spokesperson.

15. *Give it a rest.* Cool-speak for "Could you stop going on and on about this" or "Shut your mouth" or "You're being tiresome" or "Please!" or "Enough already!" It's crisp and to the point, but we should all—you know.

16. *I'm outta here.* The new pseudo-brash way of saying that "I" is leaving, with the idea that the departure or escape is well-earned and that the utterer deserves congratulations for boasting about it.

17. *It's not a level playing field.* Or, "It's not fair." The overuse of this sports metaphor is increasingly unfair to many other ways of saying the same thing.

18. *Cut me a little slack.* A plea to let one off just this once, to go easy, to make an exception, to bend the rules. Interestingly, it means what "Give me a break" used to mean.

19. *You better believe it!* Another used-to-death pat exclamation like "You got it!" and "All right!" The old-fashioned "You bet!" and "Damn right!" had more charm.

20. *He/she just doesn't get it.* Obviously, there continue to

be millions of dense and dumb people in the world who don't apprehend or catch on (regarding their own shortcomings, this usually implies), but this flip comment is particularly bumptious and self-serving.

21. *He's/she's history.* A nicely to-the-point expression for writing somebody off, but by now as fresh as a rerun sitcom line.

22. *Don't ask.* A fair enough anticipatory request, but it's being heard a little too much and said a little too quickly. Maybe there are just too many people who want to ask these days, but more likely there are too many people who feel good giving off a dry and laconic two-word warning.

23. *Have you got a problem with that?* Certainly useful. This can be asked, with eyebrows cocked, in many different situations, from deciding to use a gas station rest room to telling your spouse you're going to night school. It's usually less a request for permission than an announcement of self-permission or a veiled challenge.

24. *Trust me.* The rule is very simple here. The more frequently or emphatically one uses this expression, the less one should be trusted.

25. *Absolutely.* If too many people like to begin sentences with *Hopefully . . . ,* too many like to respond to anything, *Absolutely.* It's remarkable that this has become the most popular declaration of solid agreement, since all coast-to-coast sportscasters use *No doubt about it* or *No question about it* every third or fourth sentence.

The deliberately misspelled word in last week's column was *millenium.* It's *millennium.*

SLANG SHOT

WORD OF THE WEEK: *framis*—comically nonsensical double-talk

QUOTE OF THE WEEK: "A writer must teach himself that the basest of all things is to be afraid."
—WILLIAM FAULKNER

There are certain types of people who are always cruising for a verbal bruising. How are you at making up your own slang for some creative name-calling?

Necessity is the mother of word invention, too, and there are times when the dictionary just fails us. We have a very definite meaning nagging at us but no word for it. Or we even have a very definite person nagging at us but no word for him or her.

Maybe you want a term for the guy who chews food with his mouth open, a sight to take your own appetite away. Or for the person who eats so primly and neatly, it makes you want to eat with your mouth open. Or for the individual who slowly and openly excavates his nostril with a finger while discussing insurance policies or religion with you. Or for the person who is never on time. Or . . .

Sure, we have lots of adjectives for people with habits we don't like—*inconsiderate, rude, selfish, vulgar, gross.* But if you know any nouns (called agent nouns) for the particular beings mentioned above, you should be writing this column.

As extensive as American slang is, there aren't enough terms to cover all the malefactors, or open-mouthed eaters, fussy eaters, and always-late people, in English. We need more colorful substantives for the more particularized types of rude, crude, and lewd people out there.

We have *boor, vulgarian, slob, philistine,* and the like for objectionably low humans, but such words are rather general, unspecific. What about somebody who wears too much makeup? Who leaves the toilet seat up? What can you call a person who has a grating voice? Or one who hogs all of the bed while sleeping? Or a married couple with horrible taste in furnishings and decor?

Time for your own personal slang shot: an open invitation from Mr. Wordwizard to make up your own slanguage. (Curious to note, there is an old word, *langrage,* for a kind of shot, like schrapnel, used in naval warfare.)

Slang, as you know, is our informal, colorful, and get-real idiom. You make it by grabbing at a salient or amusing aspect of the something or someone. You combine two words or turn a clever phrase—or create a colorful epithet. You expose and debunk in a sporty way. For example, what would be a slang term for slang itself? In Lester Berrey and Melvin Van den Bark's wonderful *American Thesaurus of Slang,* you'll find among slangy terms for the word *attaboy language, jazz jargon,* and *gum-chewing words.*

Or should we call the enormous area of English slang *wiseacreage?*

"All slang," wrote G. K. Chesterton, "is metaphor, and all metaphor is poetry."

But it's perhaps people with unfortunate (for others) ways, habits, and mannerisms who most beg to be slang-dered with a descriptive term.

To zero in on our fellow gross creatures, we need some playful, earthy epithets. You know, more words along the lines of *half pint, blockhead, clodhopper, bonehead, dirt bag, slimeball, buttinsky, penny pincher, stuffed shirt, flannel mouth, panty-waist, doormat, drip, poker face, fuddy-duddy, queer duck, stick-in-the-mud, bluenose, blabbermouth, clock stopper, bag of wind, carrottop, airhead.* . . . There are many obscene epithets, too, but why be foully off-color when you can be cleanly colorful?

Here are some people-pegging neologisms for your consideration and inspiration (you can do better than these).

verbal turtle (or *syllabore*). A slow talker.

spritzfritz. A person who spits or sprays when talking.

sentence crasher. A person always interrupting.

promotion frisker. A male (boss) sexual harasser.

orange panther (or *spring turkey*). A older woman who dresses young.

gray blade. An older man who dresses young.

ghast-mask. A woman who wears too much makeup.

snappy laundry bag. A man whose clothes are always rumpled.

aerobomaniac. A physical exercise addict.

flab accountant. Person always trying new diets.

dermis thermos (or *dripsickle*). A sweaty person.

parking lot tourist. A person with no appreciation of nature.

funnies tragedy. An adult comic book reader.

shoe tongue. A person who always says the wrong thing.

no-showoff (or *clockwork lemon*). A person never on time.

fashion twitch. A man always adjusting his clothing.

privy-crat. A bathroom reader.

crack shot. A person always scratching his or her posterior.

hair conductor. A woman always playing with her hair.

profile spastic. A woman always jerking her head and hair.

cosy yogi (or *carpet frog*). A person who likes to sit cross-legged on the floor.

Wrigley Holstein. A continual gum chewer.

lunge runt. A short person who takes big springy steps.

pockpickitpuss. A person with bad skin.

loonytooth. A person with bad crooked teeth.

splatprat. A person with huge buttocks.

perfume sale. One who wears too much scent.

bed-eagler. A person who hogs the whole bed.

ample turnover. A person who takes most of the covers.

moonlight rhino. A noisy snorer.

pyrosomniac. A person who smokes in bed.

cuteness actuary. A girl always talking about boys.

bodyshop guide. A boy always talking about girls.

chompanzee. A noisy food chewer.

help-your-selfish. A person who takes selfish food portions.

chow crane. An impolite reacher at the table.

fridge commuter. A chronic between-meals snacker.

brain drill. A person who keeps one on the telephone.

lint commando. A compulsive housecleaner.

dustball kicker. A terrible housekeeper.

dyspeptician (or *frozen potholder*). A terrible cook.

jack-of-all-thumbs (or *domoplegic*). A person who can't fix anything.

kitsch-kouple. A couple with terrible taste.

Twinkie Hostess. A mother who feeds her children junk food.

repast master. A father always critical of the food served him.

head-hookey star (or *study-duddy*). A child who balks at doing homework.

mouth-offspring. A child who talks back to his or her parents.

overachieftains. Parents who push children to excel.

fair-weather master. One who hates to walk the dog.

ear squall. A person with a grating voice.

kitty cooer. An insufferable cat lover.

Don Juan-and-on (or *conquestador*). A sexual-conquest
   braggart.

splash-in-the-pan. A lousy dishwasher.

throbbing wallflower. A person always wanting others to
   fix him or her up.

frog kisser. A woman who can't meet the right man.

maypole choreographer. A male who gives precise love-
   making instructions.

foreplay stewardess. A female who gives precise love-
   making instructions.

absentee ironing board. A poor female lover.

sorry sack. A poor male lover.

shake-and-fake biscuit. A woman who fakes orgasms.

seizure salad. A sexually responsive female.

primp simp. A man overly vain about his body.

unsyncopath. A person always breaking appointments.

But these only scratch the surface. There are so many
nounal descriptives that our dictionaries lack for particular types of or excuses for people. The person who
never says thank you. The person who sneaks or breaks
into supermarket lines. The person who takes up two
seats. The person who steals your parking space. . . .

How about you taking some slang shots by coining a
few terms for types of people, people who deserve to be
pegged by labels of the brashly informal variety? For
inspiration, leaf through a dictionary or, better yet, a
dictionary of slang. (Four well-known ones are by Went-
worth and Flexner, Spears, Chapman, and Lighter.)

As the three authors of a 1927 book *The Science of
Society* said, "A people who are prosperous and happy,
optimistic and progressive, will produce much slang; it is
a case of play; they amuse themselves with the language."

The deliberately misspelled word in last week's column was *forego*. It's *forgo*.

ENOUGH ENUF

Word of the Week: *slurvian*—carelessly slurred and sloppy speech

Quote of the Week: "Try not to let phrases discourage words."

—Jean Rostand

I had a nightmare last night, and it was an ortho-graphic, or spelling-related, nightmare. It was caused not by something I ate but by Councilman Bryll's recent proposal to simplify the spelling of public signs around Woofton.

Actually, it was not a nightmare.

It was a nitemare.

Councilman Henry Bryll has said English spelling is far too complicated for most people and that we should lead the way—or leed the way—in Woofton by spelling all road and store signs phonetically for easy under-standing. He has suggested, for example, that "Reduce Speed" should be "Redoose Speed." "Slippery When Wet" should be "Slipree Wen Wet." "Reserved for Handicapped" should be "Rezerved 4 Handeekapt."

Jest wot we nede. I won't go into all the reasons here why redoing our English spelling is a pie-in-the-sky no-tion. All right, I'll mention a few.

Simplified spelling would be too complicated. The new spellings would obscure the interesting other-lan-

guage origins of our English words. There would be a
special problem with homophones, our words pronounced the same but spelled differently and having different meanings. There would be the problem of altering people's names and place names. And what would
become of the centuries of, the billions of, convention-
ally spelled books and other documents we rely on today?

I'll also mention that it's been reported that Councilman Bryll failed spelling repeatedly in grammar school
and that he worked too long in the field of advertising.

No, this all aside, the worst thing about public and
commercial respelling is its pseudo-cuteness. It's America's visual baby talk, and we never seem to outgrow it.

You know those spelling-compressed words like *nite,
lite, glo, kleen,* and *luv.* The squealingly cute-ified English of consumer-wooing America, from highway bill-
boards, to eatery and motel names, to so many appli-
ances, household food products, and just about anything
buyable, play-withable, or eatable by children, from toys
to cereals. Actually, it's a kind of spelling that makes
children of us all, or tries to.

These infantalized spellings are phoneticisms, or phonetic (or fonetic) spellings, or spellings preshrunk for
pronunciation: *koffee shop, dri-kleener, laff-riot.* . . .

It's as if somebody were forcing oral speech on the
written word.

You may not know that the best-known of all U.S.
expressions derives from two words antically misspelled.
O.K. or *okay,* that Americanism of Americanisms that
the world can't do without, comes—a debated issue finally solved by the great language scholar Allen Walker
Read—from "oll korrect."

The chief traits of this visual letter-al baby talk are
lone or final vowels that nakedly jump out at you and
seem to jingle (as well as doubled ones, as in *jooce* instead of *juice)* and plonking consonants, especially *k*'s
replacing *c*'s or *ck*'s.

Why is this cartoony spelling so quintessentially

American? Your guess is as good as mine. Echoes of the old spelling illiteracy of our frontier nineteenth-century days? In our hung-up-on-being-young culture, a sign of a wish to be not just youthful but actual children? Sheer advertising space-saving and getting the meaning across supersimply—bludgeoning salesmanship? Or a perverse desire to exterminate all silent or unpronounced vowels and consonants in English?

In my nightmare—nitemare—I found myself driving through a new Woofton.

It was Woofton after the invasion of the alphabet switchers.

It was worse than the Twilight Zone. It was the Twilite Zone. The kiddee-writers had taken over and divied up all the signs in town.

I was driving to Ventner's Books, my favorite Woofton bookstore, but planned first to stop for an appointment with my chiropractor and pick up some supplies at Smither's Stationery Store.

But even before I reached Main Street, I could see that Woofton was a different Woofton. Schwartz Opticians was now X-Eye-Ting Optiks, and upstairs from it was something called D-Duck-Ted Tax Services. Old Mr. Williams's glazier supply store sign now read C-Thru Glass, and in the old empty lot next to it were now the Kreem of the Krop Cafe, No-Swet Air Konditioning, and U-Bet State Lottery.

I turned onto Main Street. All the familiar storefronts and signs looked different.

Miller's Storage had become Sta-Put Storidge, two doors away from Truss-T Orthotiks and Eh-One Hearing Aids. The large wooden house of the Colonial Funeral Home was still there, but the sign outside said Morehead's Redi-Bodi Funeralama. I broke into a sweat and turned right toward the office of my chiropractor. A large plastic skeleton with a happy face stood on the lawn and now read Krackling Kiropraktors.

I couldn't stop. I made a U-turn, but thought of it secretly as a you-turn, and sped down Main Street again toward Smither's Stationery Store—but not before I passed a whole new and unfamiliar mall.

There was Nutz and Boltz Hardware, Jiffee Arkiteks, Pokey's Akupunkture, and the Timely Taxee Service, which I knew was not Chinese. There was the Boro Hall, except that it was now the Burro Hall, and in front of the Woofton Museum was a new neon sign with a cow reading Woofton Moo-Z-Um. Before I reached Smither's Stationery Store I knew what to expect, and I was right. It was now Rite-Rite Pay-Per-'n'-Pen, and right next to it was Gig-O-Lo Eskort Agency, Skin-Flint Dermatology, Kutesy-Poo Diaper Service, and Pop-'n'-Drop Gun Shoppe.

Down the next street was what had been my favorite record store. The sign over it now read The Music Luvuh. Right next to it was a redone maternity fashions shop, Mutha Kuva, and the Faw Luvahs and Othuhs Greeting Cod Staw.

Panicking, I headed for the outskirts of town. There was St. John's Church, only now it was St. Jon's. Next to it was the Sistuhs of Mercee Konvent. I knew I wasn't in Kansas anymore. I headed back into town. Would the nitemare have gone away by now?

I needed an island of sanity. I needed my beloved Ventner's Books. It was not to be. I pulled into the parking lot of the newly painted building, and it was now Hi-Q Skolarlee Books. I screamed and woke myself up.

The whole thing was like a bad spell.

The deliberately misspelled word in last week's column was *schrapnel*. It's *shrapnel*. (Phonetic spellings in the above column do *not* count as candidates for the prize awarded next week.)

WHAT'S A CAHOOT?

WORD OF THE WEEK: *faux naif*—falsely or phonily artless, simple, or naïve

QUOTE OF THE WEEK: "There's nothing to writing. All you do is sit down at a typewriter and open a vein."

—RED SMITH

You've no doubt had occasion in life to take umbrage at something. But what's an umbrage? Do you know the meaning of *kilter*? How about *fettle* or *shrift*? What's a *tenterhook*? Or a *cahoot*?

Chances are you have a vague notion of the meanings of these somewhat archaic words, and that when asked to define them, you immediately associate each with a particular phrase: *to take umbrage at, out of kilter, in fine fettle, to give* (someone) *short shrift, on tenterhooks, in cahoots with.* And with good reason. Such words are today virtually one-idiom-only words, having almost no life in the English language beyond the discrete phrase they've become a part of, like fossilized insects preserved in amber. (You will find other definitions for some of them in dictionaries, but here's a little lexical secret: When a dictionary adds parenthetically that a word is "usually used" or is "chiefly used" in a certain idiom, you can bet it is virtually always used in that certain idiom.)

These—along with *dint, cropper, offing, druthers,*

hackles and *dander, behest, roughshod, brunt, tizzy, willies, huff* (as a noun), *lurch* (as a noun), *throe,* and others —are akin to what in grammar are called defective words. A defective word is not a broken or harshly judged one. Rather, it is one lacking the usual varied forms or inflections (the most notable defectives in English are such modal verbs as *may, must, can,* and *ought*). Or, to borrow an analogy from football, words like *kilter* and *fettle* are special-team players, not all-round or all-game players.

Did you ever stop to think about such phrasally protected words? We use them in these stock expressions, but we probably couldn't define the key word by itself. Now you will be able to—at least, some of them—with this quick little roundup of some idiom-locked words, each of which we'll separate out.

You'll note that they're all nouns. Notice anything else most of them have in common? It is that the idioms express pained or distressed emotional states—being on tenterhooks, in the throes of, in a huff, in high dudgeon, in a tizzy, getting one's dander up, making one's hackles rise, taking umbrage, or (the opposite) being in fine fettle. One can only conjecture why this is the case with so many of them.

Being on tenterhooks is being on edge or in a state of suspense. So what's a tenterhook? It's a hook or bent nail used to stretch newly woven clothes on the frame called a tenter.

To take umbrage is to take offense or be miffed. The dictionary will tell you that the word *umbrage,* from the Latin *umbra,* is used alone to mean shade or foliage, but we all know that the only sense we encounter is somebody taking it. The idiom's meaning evolved from the sense of feeling overshadowed or threatened.

There's nothing strange about the word *roughshod,* which refers to a horse having horseshoes with projecting nails or points. But in the general English of dudes, it appears only in the phrase *to ride roughshod over,* meaning to treat imperiously, harshly, or cruelly.

What's a dint, or rather, what's dint? *By dint of* something is by virtue of or because of the fact of something, *dint* meaning "force or power." It comes from Old Norse words for "blow" and "to fall" and is, the dictionary tells us, related to an Albanian word *gdhent* that means "I chop wood."

The brunt of something, as in *to bear the brunt of,* is the main force, impact, thrust, or stress of it, which is exactly what the word sounds like it should mean. Curiously, *brunt* may derive from a Middle English term for sexual assault and be related to an Old English word meaning "heat" or "itching."

A throe is a sharp bolt of emotion, a spasm or pang, but we seem to hear it only in the plural. To be *in the throes of* something is to be undergoing a kind of physical or emotional convulsion or struggle. *Throe* comes from an Old English word meaning "to suffer" or "to be in pain."

When we talk about *leaving somebody in the lurch,* we might guess that a lurch is an unsteady, lurching position. Not so. The term originally meant a position in certain games (such as cribbage) in which the loser is losing very badly or scores no points at all. It derives from a Middle French word *lourch,* for "game," although the adjective meant "discomfited."

Behoove is another odd word. When we say *it behooves* someone to do something, we mean that it is advised or necessary, or incumbent upon them, to do that something. The word comes from a Middle English one meaning "to need." Actually, your dictionary will tell you there is a word *behoof,* meaning "use, benefit, or advantage," but when's the last time you heard anybody talking about a behoof for something? In the same area of meaning is *behest,* as in our expression *at the behest of,* meaning "at the command or urging of." A behest is a bit stronger in force than a request, and it goes back to a Middle English word for "promise."

Our idioms *to get one's dander up* and *to make one's hackles rise* are also close in meaning: to become angry and to be made angry, respectively. Dander is the loose scales shed from an animal's coat or feathers that often cause allergic reactions in people, and yes, it is related to the word *dandruff*. Hackles, plural, are the erectile hairs on the back of the neck of certain animals, such as dogs, that stiffen when the animal is hostilely aroused. It's better to be in fine (or good) fettle, meaning "to be feeling tiptop," a fettle being a condition or circumstance and coming from a Middle English word meaning "to shape or prepare from."

Then there are *in the offing, to give someone short shrift, to have one's druthers,* and *to come a cropper.* What is an offing, a shrift, a druther, a cropper? We use *offing* to mean the envisioned or near future, but it's actually a nautical term for the distant band of the sea as viewed from the shore. To give someone short shrift is to give them little attention or to shortchange them in consideration, and the derivation is penal-religious. Shrift is confession to or absolution from a priest, and short shrift originally referred specifically to the brief visit of a priest to a condemned person. *Druthers,* a plural noun for a wishful, if-only-it-could-be preference, comes simply enough from the contraction *I'd rather.* *To come a cropper,* or to fail or have a bad setback, comes not from farming but from hunting, where the phrase means to take a severe fall from a horse; *cropper,* the dictionary informs us, probably comes from another idiom, *neck and crop,* meaning completely or summarily.

But not too much light can be shed on the key words in the idioms *in high dudgeon, in a tizzy, out of kilter, in a huff,* and *to give one the willies.* Lexicographers have no sure answers as to exactly where these words come from. Dudgeon is a feeling of offense or resentment, but we find it only in this cast-iron idiom and never hear of anybody being in low dudgeon. A tizzy, of course, is an anxious or distracted state of mind, a dither. The derivation of *kilter* is unknown. The word means "order or good condition" but only survives in this negative phrase, for we never speak of something being in kilter or in good kilter. *Huff may be related to puff.* It's a sulky, angry mood, but it's always preceded by *in a.* As for the willies, the idiom dictates that we never lie awake with them or suffer from them. Somebody or something always gives you the willies—the jitters or the creeps. Etymologists know this is an American expression but can't, willy-nilly, pin down the origin of *willy.*

And then there's *cahoot.* When we hear about somebody in cahoots—in league or partnership—with somebody else, we think of Old West cowboys, trekers, or even varmints. The word *cahoot* is from a French word, *cahute,* for "cabin."

So some of these curious one-idiom-only words remain a little mysterious, sort of like a verbal pig in a poke—another such phrase, and you probably aren't quite sure what a poke is. It's a small bag or sack, but don't count on using it in this sense (and being understood) other than in the phrase *a pig in a poke.*

The deliberately misspelled word in last week's column was *divied.* It's *divvied.*

TORMENTING TERMS

WORD OF THE WEEK: *ethnophaulism*—an ethnic slur

QUOTE OF THE WEEK: "Self-expression is for babies and seals, where it can be charming. A writer's business is to affect the reader."

—VINCENT MCHUGH

*E*linguation? Patibulation? Scaphism? Abandon hope, all ye who think these might be literary terms.

You know about words that can make people flinch. They'd be chiefly obscene or taboo words, the very sound or sight of which can offend. But how about words whose *meanings* can make us uncomfortable? Or should?

Unflinching, let's shine a shaky lantern at some of the dark recesses of old dictionaries, where verbal monuments to past—and present—human cruelties survive. I refer to rare, faceless-looking words for terrible deeds, most of them not found in your college dictionary. I refer to terms for types of torture and execution.

I don't want to give you cardiac arhythmia, but this will be a slightly morbid column in its unusual (but interesting) subject. Or an algogenic one, *algogenic* being a big word meaning "producing pain." But when you've read through it, you'll probably feel good. (No pain, no gain.) You'll be glad to be living in the modern twentieth-century world.

But before we start, let's make it interesting. Imagine that you're a condemned prisoner told you may choose one of three ways to be punished. You can choose between (1) elinguation, (2) patibulation, and (3) scaphism. What's your pleasure, so to speak?

Read up on your world history, and you'll realize that *torture* (or *sheer torture*) is a word we usually use too lightly today. A sermon is sheer torture, we may say, or a teasing friend is torturing you about a fabulous gift awaiting you. We talk blithely of putting the screws to somebody, the Chinese water torture, and being on the rack. When we're fiercely resistant, we say we'd rather be skinned alive, walk over hot coals, be boiled in oil, be hung (that's hanged) from the highest something, have our fingernails pulled out, be keelhauled, and so on. We're just using graphic metaphors, speaking figuratively. Figuratively—lucky for us or whomever we're talking about.

But some words in the cryptic lexicon of torture are not colorful, concrete expressions. Rather, they're cold and clinical and seem almost abstractions, devised within a merciless dungeon of their own. Words like *artuate, cangue, excarnificate, forcipation, suspercollate,* and *vivisepulture* along with the three above. Icily Latinate and scientific-sounding, such words give us—in their revealed definitions—a glimpse at the very real, not at all figurative, cruelties of past human history, from the ancient Age of Tyrants to the Middle Ages to the Inquisition to France's Reign of Terror. They are true curiosities (you're a rare bird if you know more than one or two of them) in being bloodless terms for very bloody actions. They sound medical but are all penal.

Curiously, most of these "technical" terms for methods of human cruelty don't appear even in scholarly books on the subject of torture.

If you don't want to torture somebody, you can *excarnificate* him or her. It means the same: "to torture or execute, usually by tearing the flesh." One way is by *ganching,* or impaling on stakes or hooks. (I'm going to be breezy and not dwell on these definitions.) As opposed to such less severe things as *bilboes,* a foot-locking long metal bar with sliding shackles; the *branks,* an iron form used to encase a prisoner's head with a triangular "bit" locked into the mouth (used, appropriately, to punish scolds); a *cangue,* which was a heavy square of wood that was hung around the head and usually confined the hands; a *pilliwinks,* a torture instrument used on the thumb and fingers; or a *scarpines,* a leg torture instrument. The torture of the *bastinado* was having the soles of your feet beaten mercilessly—a more focused variety of *fustigation,* or being beaten with a stick.

Execation—or blinding—has always been a method of torture. Also known, in chill technical terms, as *exoculation.* To *eluscate* somebody is to blind him or her in only one eye. To *abacinate* is to blind by means of a hot metal plate held close to the eyes.

Similarly—no, not really—there is the grisly means of death commonly known as disembowelment, except that it can also be known as *eventration* or *exenteration.* Less terminal was the use of a stake or sharpened peg for a military punishment known as *picketing,* whereby the malefactor had to hang (tied) by one arm with the bare foot resting on the point of the stake.

Are you still with me?

Cyphonism, having nothing to do with siphoning, is exposure in a pillory (the above-mentioned cangue being a kind of portable cyphonism). The loss of one's ears —how?—in a pillory was called *ear rent.*

Two torturous words you may know are *decimate* and *defenestration.* To decimate, originally, was a military punishment, determined by lot, whereby every tenth man was executed. A little luckier for the troops was *vigesimation:* every twentieth man was killed. Defenestration, mainly a humorous word, is throwing somebody out or through a window, not so much a form of torture as a brutal exit and in reality not exactly humorous. (In the 1964 movie *The Killers* you can see Lee Marvin almost defenestrate Angie Dickinson: he hangs her out briefly headfirst for a sudden overview. Later, when he aims a gun at her and she pleads for her life, he says wearily, "Lady, I just don't have the time.")

What about suffocating, hanging, cutting someone's throat? To suffocate (especially in order to obtain a cadaver for medical purposes) is to *burke*. To hang someone is to *suspercollate* them. Possibly worse, certainly slower, than hanging was the *strappado,* being hoisted by a rope that tied the wrists behind one's back and then being allowed to fall suddenly the length of the rope. To cut someone's throat (or to strangle) is to *jugulate. Fusillation* is the old word for capital punishment by shooting, and the *fusillade* is the firing squad. Being burned at the stake (or the "ceremony" accompanying that pronouncement on a heretic) was called the *auto-da-fé.* Better to be appreciated in the role of a human sacrifice and suffer *immolation.* To skin somebody was to *flay* them; regrettably, that simple word was applied to human beings as well as animals, often when they were alive.

A capital way to be mercifully free of torture, of course, is to lose your head. Decapitation or beheading is also known as *decollation* (not to be confused with décolletage) or *kephalotomy.* (In Rome the bodies of decapitated criminals or martyrs were placed, presumably headless, on an *equuleus,* a kind of fork or gibbet.)

Forcipation, not forced feeding, was torture by nipping with pincers. If you wanted to get stoned—literally, meaning to the death—you'd ask to be *lapidated,* which you might prefer to *vivisepulture,* or being buried alive, also known as *defossion.* A lot less lonely a form of death was the *noyade,* or mass drowning, as took place in Nantes, France, during the Reign of Terror.

These fates are bad enough, even in nice Latinish-type terms. But you could have done, or been done to, worse.

You could have been *artuated,* or torn limb from limb, if not *cruciated,* or crucified, or become the chosen one for *mactation,* the killing of a sacrificial victim. You could have been subjected to the *scavenger's daughter,* a torture instrument that compressed the body until blood was forced from the nostrils and ears "and sometimes the hands and feet," as one source puts it. This horrible squashing torture was also known, in French, as *peine fort et dure* ("strong and hard pain")—a rare term but one used casually by novelist Vladimir Nabokov in *Lolita.* Or you could have been incarcerated in the *Sicilian Bull,* a brass bull inside which the victim was roasted alive so his "roars" could come out the shaped mouth of the human kettle—a toy of the ancient Sicilian tyrant Phalaris. (The word *philotheoparoptesism* was coined by English novelist Thomas Love Peacock for the slow cooking of those with whom the Church was displeased.) Or there was the *iron maiden,* a kind of hinged metal mummy case, with long spikes in its front door, for living tenants.

Or you could have been *drawn and quartered.* There's an expression you've probably heard. What you may not know is that the drawing and quartering were done before the victim died. One was first dragged by a horse or a cart, then had one's limbs tied to four horses who were then driven in four directions, and then . . . Sounds a fate quite worse than *anthropophagy,* or cannibalism.

But let's leave bad enough alone. All that remains is the answer to our opening quiz: Would you rather suffer (1) elinguation, (2) patibulation, or (3) scaphism?

If you choose elinguation, you'd save your life but have your tongue cut out.

Patibulation, like suspercollation, is death by hanging.

Scaphism would definitely be your most unfortunate choice here. It is the term for an ancient Persian method of torment, whereby the unfortunate was confined in a trough or boatlike container, with his or her head and limbs smeared with honey, and exposed to the sun and all interested insects. History shows that this torture, unfortunately, did not go out of date with the ancient

Persians; and you may have heard of variations of it— for example, employing stakes near anthills—practiced from Asia and the Middle East to North and South America.

If this column has been painful for you to read, think how torturous (not to be confused with tortuous) it was to research and write (and how many details I've spared you). In life, we occasionally hear the expression, "Well, they're only words." In the case of torture terminology, it's not the words, it's the meanings that offend. Let's hope the day comes when they are only words.

The deliberately misspelled word in last week's column was *trekers*. It's *trekkers*.

CEREAL KILLINGS

WORD OF THE WEEK: *Aesopian*—having a secret meaning to those in the know

QUOTE OF THE WEEK: "This morning I took out a comma and this afternoon I put it back again."

—OSCAR WILDE

How about a verbal recipe—for just the right language ingredients a food manufacturer might use to market a cereal called, say, Fiblets? Or one called, say, Kokoa Korpses?

You may already know how to recognize empty-calorie food. Do you also know empty-calorie language when you see it?

There is writing as a craft, and there is writing as a craftiness.

To go into your local supermarket is to have an adventure not only in product selection but in false—or at least fibbing—advertising. I'm talking about verbal packaging. Language can be treacherous when it's being used to sell something, and for the informed purchaser shopping becomes a kind of decoding operation. And to learn every Madison Avenue trick in the book, you can't do better than to spend some time reading those boxes containing "healthy" breakfast cereals that come all the way from the graineries of the Midwest.

Numerous foods can be called American, but breakfast cereals are beyond that. They're Americana. Decades of advertising slogans, endorsements, and double-talk have made sure we associate cereals with robust health, energy, and snap, crackle, and pop to start the day.

Or should we really associate most of them with sneaky dollops of sugar?

All marketed food products are worth being suspicious about, but cereals are especially so since American children are the prime consumer target of the manufacturers. Behind the healthful claims of most of the wheat and oat and bran flakes or grains lies a lot of corn syrup. So the cereal market is a battleground for the hearts and tummies of television-age youngsters.

It's time for a little consumer-protection look at cereal killings, or the profitable English of false advertising. (As Cary Grant, playing an advertising executive, says in Alfred Hitchcock's *North by Northwest,* "In advertising, there's no such thing as a lie. There's only expedient exaggeration.") And for a few thoughts as to how you might sell your own fictitious unnutritious cereal.

From those big colorful boxes, it's clear that breakfast cereals are the Disneyland of alimentary half-truths and kute kalories. Your typical cereal package is emblazoned with surefire adjectives, boffo superlatives, and clever and not-even-so-clever hedging or weasel words. To say little of how misleadingly oversize most air-filled cereal boxes are. It is said that they take up more (unnecessary) space than any other food product sold in a supermarket.

Weasel words are those that neutralize or make essentially meaningless the words they're paired up with, or they are cosmetic terms that are empty or at best misleading. They're subversive qualifiers, or semantic additives. If you call something an "authentic replica," *authentic* is a weasel word. Other common weaselly expressions are "helps to," "acts to," and "almost like." A close cousin to the weasel word is the absolute or dangling comparative, a comparison that is slyly incomplete, such as "Has more nutrients" (more than what?) or "Makes clothes brighter" (brighter than what?). Not surprisingly, this is also called the agency comparative. Every consumer should be aware of weasel words and agency comparatives and, more important, be able to spot them. (Show me a person who fondles false language, and I'll show you a meaning-molester.)

Some cereal packages stress nutrition and good health alone (with, say, a background picture of the Swiss Alps, an autumnal harvest scene, or fruited plains and purple mountains' majesty), but more of them show perky cartoon characters or animals, bright colors, and lots of jumpy but unnutritious exclamation points.

All to hide the fact that the cereal may be practically grain-scented candy, if not the candy parents warn their children never to accept from strangers.

Four of the favorite words in cereal advertising are *fortified, enriched, sugar free* (or *sugarless),* and *natural.* A fortified cereal contains some nutritious supplements, but these other terms mean a lot less, as William Lutz points out in *Doublespeak.* A so-called enriched cereal is one that has the vitamins, minerals, or protein restored that it lost in processing—it is merely back where it started from nutritionally. A sugar-free cereal ("No refined sugar!") has no sucrose, or table sugar, but it may contain instead fruit sugar (fructose), dextrose (corn sugar), honey, glucose, or another sweetener with just as many calories.

As for the word *natural,* it means nothing, nor—so far —must it legally. (A case challenging its use is currently pending in the State of California.) A cereal may contain thickeners, emulsifiers, flavor enhancers, preservatives, or certain chemicals and still be called natural. How many American consumers are aware of this? Or that, as Zena Block notes in *It's All On the Label,* as a rule of thumb sweetened cereals designed to appeal to children contain 45 to 55 percent sugar?

Truth, when it comes to food, lies in that list of ingredients. With cereals, the first or second of those ingredients is more often than not "fructose," "sucrose," "corn syrup," or "sugar."

Cereal advertising also often tries to have it both ways. Something is reliably sweet—but has "less" sugar. It's healthful and nutritious—but super-fruity-sweet or cocoa-covered.

How do the cereal killers exploit the English language on cereal packages? Let us count the ways.

1. The use of tried-and-true adjectives such as *delicious, nutritious, tasty, scrumptious, essential,* and *wholesome.* Call them not unbiased value judgments of the manufacturer.

2. Emphasizing what isn't an ingredient—and possibly isn't at all likely to be. No salt, no cholesterol, no artificial something, no preservatives—or no rat poison. This emphasis, of course, distracts from the calorific things that *are* the ingredients. It's an American-as-apple-pie variation of the old *ignoratio elenchi* fallacy, or the stressing of what is irrelevant. Similarly, there's emphasizing what hasn't been "added": "No added sugar." "No added flavors."

3. The use of the all-important word *natural.* The health-food revolution has left this nice English word quite hollow, but evidently shoppers still want to read it somewhere on a box or can. It has a reassuring "grass roots" ring to it. "With natural ingredients" (if not necessarily good ones). "100% natural." "Natural fruit flavors." It's all naturally meaningless.

4. The use of the word *fiber.* "High fiber." "A good source of fiber." How many cereals don't offer some sort of fiber?

5. The use of a line such as "Kids love it!" (or "Kids love 'em!") or of the word *crunchy* or *krunchy.*

6. Zesty nonsense, such as "Great fun!" "Bite-size!" "Great taste!" "Easy directions!"

7. Box-front distractions or premium or gift offers: "Free with purchase (see back for details) . . ." "Save 50% on . . ."

8. Emphasizing that the product can be a snack, too.

Language matters aside, it also helps if the units of cereal have a distinctive or cute and completely unnecessary shape—say, of a teddy bear or a friendly great white shark. (The more the manufacturers can make the cereal units resemble a cute creature, a chocolate marshmallow cookie, a potato chip, a danish pastry, or a double chocolate fudge sundae, the better.)

With these points in mind, you'll know just how you might go about packaging two hypothetical new breakfast cereals. (Most breakfast cereals would be better for you if they were 80 percent hypothetical.) Let's call one Fun Fiblets and the other Kokoa Korpses.

Fun Fiblets, shaped to be able to form exclamation points (some pieces long grains, others dotlike), are pink pieces of crystallized sugar dipped in wheat germ and processed with artificial color, preservatives, and other chemicals.

The colorful Fun Fiblets cereal box shows dancing exclamation points in different colors. It also says: "The skrumptious emphatic way to start the day!" "Healthily edulcorated [an old word meaning "sweetened"], and contains no bacon fat." "No added cholesterol." "100% Natural!" "Virtual source of fiber!" "Kids gobble 'em!" "More ingredients than other leading brands!" "Zappy fun!"

Kokoa Korpses, shaped like stiff human bodies, are made from brown sugar dipped in sawdust and chocolate syrup and chemically enhanced.

The Kokoa Korpses cereal box shows colorful cartoon monsters leaving a trail of cute corpses. It also says: "A scary treat with monster chocolate taste!" "Krunch bite-sized korpse kubes!" "No white sugar, salt, or pepper added." "Fortified with pure sucrose!" "Great as Kannibal Snacks!"

Fun Fiblets and Kokoa Korpses are fictitious, but only a little more than the names has been changed to protect the guilty. Some of those cereal producers know how to sugarcoat the truth. Or is it how to nutritionalize sugar?

English, like cereal, isn't something just to be taken in. You should look closely at its ingredients. Language is like nutrition, and words misused or overused are its empty calories.

The deliberately misspelled word in last week's column was *arhythmia*. It's *arrhythmia*.

DEVILISH DEFINING

WORD OF THE WEEK: *griffonage*—illegible handwriting

QUOTE OF THE WEEK: "Planning to write is not writing. Outlining . . . researching . . . talking to people about what you're doing, none of that is writing. Writing is writing."

—E. L. DOCTOROW

November, n. The eleventh twelfth of a weariness.
Ultimatum, n. In diplomacy, a last demand before resorting to concessions.
Apologize, v. To lay the foundation for a future offense.

Are you ready to test the Curmudgeon Quotient of your thinking and writing skills?

For acquiring an understanding of words, there are dictionary definitions—and there are perverse definitions.

Since nobody ever said dictionary meanings had to be angelic, the American satirical writer Ambrose Bierce (1842–1914?) decided it might be interesting to make them thoroughly devilish. And so he gave us in 1906 the classic *The Devil's Dictionary* (originally, *The Cynic's Word Book),* from which the above definitions come. Bierce served in the Civil War, lived in London, and worked as a West Coast journalist before disappearing in Mexico, not before also writing some dark short stories.

But it's "Bitter Bierce's" witty and positively negative
definitions of things for which he is best known today.
Most of the definitions are little masterpieces of ironic
writing. (They have spawned many imitators and
updaters, and imitating Bierce is nothing at all to be
ashamed of.) Though the hollowness of contemporary
politics was a recurrent target, Bierce's definitions went
further and struck deeper than that.

Some of his barbed denotations don't "come off."
They are overlong, intellectually or metaphorically
strained, or too overripely compacted or congested to
be absorbed—they burst at the seams with admonishing,
know-it-all bloviation and read as the very self-styled
poses of a crank. But most of the definitions are bits of
brilliantly pickled wisdom, brilliant because of the almost dessicated keenness of the writing. Bierce was a
learned man, as the often obscure literary, scientific,
and other allusions in the definitions show. But however
recondite—and humorous—many of them are, the best
are like surgical knife thrusts. From startling angles,
they puncture sanctimony, hypocrisy, folly, and pretension.

And they do it through Bierce's masterly use of the
English language—which is our angle here. Bierce defined language, by the way, as "the music with which we
charm the serpents guarding another's treasure."

Can you write a devil's definition?

Everybody takes a crack at making a pun or composing a limerick now and then. Why not a caustic definition? Look at Bierce's denotational witticisms, and
you'll see it's a challenge to take a fresh—very fresh—
viewpoint on a person, thing, practice, character quality,
or term that isn't or shouldn't be all it's cracked up to
be. To compose a devil's definition is an exercise in
sharpness of perception and an ability to counterbal-
ance or play with words; in compressing your own take
on something in a few very well chosen words: the exact
and best words, the absolute minimum of words, the
perfect order in which to arrange them.

Definitions, in general, are really formalized sentence fragments, almost like careful entries in a log. They are little straight-faced, stand-back explanations. The best of the Biercean definitions are little explanations—stand-back ones indeed—pumped full of enough irony to kill a horse. (Irony, in case you've forgotten, is the sly use of words to express something quite other from what they literally say; the wry opinion glowers beneath the innocent surface.)

Devilish definitions, with their clever twists, are a form of stylistic treachery. In form they are straight, formal, and informational, but in substance they are subversive. They're flat understatement (in rectitudinous rhythm and tone) harboring explosive overstatement (in condemnation or cynicism). And devising one or two of them is *a wonderful test of your thinking and writing skills,* not to mention of your built-in bushwa detector. It is a nicely small format for word play, clever word order, rhetorical tricks and surprises. It's a chance to be a debunking miniaturist and compose cosmic one-liners.

Here, point of view—or pose—is important. To have a go at a subversive definition, assume the role of an omniscient prankster. A few examples of Bierce definitions illustrate how he does what he does.

The main thing is to reverse the usual or expectable point of view. If you're defining a negative or deplored quality or thing, define it in terms that are positive or admirable (but with that twist). If it is large, describe it as small; if surprising, make it predictable; if petty, define it as grand. And so forth. (*Accident,* n. An inevitable occurrence due to the action of immutable natural laws. *Abstainer,* n. A weak person who yields to the temptation of denying himself a pleasure. *Uxoriousness,* n. A perverted affection that has strayed to one's own wife.)

Or find a good metaphor and run with it. (*Adage,* n. Boned wisdom for weak teeth. *Husband,* n. One who, having dined, is charged with the care of the plate. *Kill,* v. To create a vacancy without nominating a successor.)

Or make a comparison or equation with something

unexpected. (*Envy,* n. Emulation adapted to the meanest capacity. *Guillotine,* n. A machine that makes a Frenchman shrug his shoulders with good reason.)

Or use a tongue-in-cheek conceited or blindly egotistic point of view. (*Discussion,* n. A method of confirming others in their errors. *Absurdity,* n. A statement of belief manifestly inconsistent with one's own opinion.)

Or hinge everything on wordplay, a turning and returning of a phrase or the reuse of a word or its meaning with a surprising twist. (*Backbite,* v. To speak of a man as you find him when he can't find you. *Convent,* n. A place of retirement for women who wish for leisure to meditate upon the vice of idleness. *Critic,* n. A person who boasts himself hard to please because nobody tries to please him.)

Or write a definition that begins innocently enough but has a stinger in its tail. (*Longanimity,* n. The disposition to endure injury with meek forbearance while maturing a plan of revenge. *Labor,* n. One of the processes by which A acquires property for B.)

There are rhetoric terms for the various stylistic devices Bierce uses, but you don't need terms to craft pithy units of wry lexicography. You need only adopt a nicely jaundiced starting point and hit upon just the right angle or point of comparison to proceed.

To inspire you, here are some Wordwizard devilish definitions:

Advertising, *n.* A commercial strategy whereby a company proves quality of product by quantity of lies.

American language, *n.* A lively dialect of British speech errors.

Anonymity, *n.* Accidental modesty.

Apology, *n.* A regret timed perfectly too late.

Applause, *n.* A response emphatically declarative, collectively imperative, and basically questionable.

Argument, *n.* The point at which two people joined in a quest for truth plant their feet and realize each has already found it.

Arouse, *v.* To give rise to another's intentions.

Autopsy, *n.* Open-death surgery.

Bore, *n.* One who commands the detention of all.

Capital punishment, *n.* A criminal case removed to a higher court.

Castration, *n.* A sudden loss affecting the mass of the privates, the volume of the voice, and the size of the public.

Commission, *n.* A deserved percentage of an exploitation.

Connoisseur, *n.* An expert in superfluous appreciation.

Conscience, *n.* The catch, before you've even been caught.

Credulity, *n.* Wishful blinking.

Cuckold, *n.* A silent partner in a new merger.

Elevator, *n.* A gathering place for embarrassed strangers.

Evangelism, *n.* Doing good upon somebody.

Faith, *n.* The art of fitting the knots through the loopholes.

Faux pas, *n.* A real botch you wish had been in French.

Free-association, *n.* Nonstop irrelevance.

Growing-up, *n.* The process of living-down.

Heredity, *n.* A lifelong excuse carried to its earliest extreme.

Life, *n.* A long lie leading to a sudden truth.

Modesty, *n.* Passive arrogance.

Panel discussion, *n.* The bobbing of closed minds in conversational openings.

Passion, *n.* Where two first sights successfully outrace two second thoughts.

Pedant, *n.* One making a nuisance of a nuance.

Photogenic, *adj.* Preferable in two dimensions.

Poll, *n.* A statistical investigation of how people will vote after they've read about the statistical investigation.

Preposterous, *adj.* Unfairly relevant.

Psychiatrist, *n.* A notary private who certifies autobiographical excuses.

Researcher, *n.* An accessory after the fact.

Reviewer, *n.* A writer in critical condition.

Saint, *n.* A promoted peasant or forgiven cleric, usually on the basis of something he saw in a weak moment.

Second honeymoon, *n.* Another desperate attempt to have a first one.

Self-confidence, *n.* Life's only practical illusion.

Self-made man, *n.* One who had admirably overcome an ignorant upbringing in order to be proud of it.

Sex, *n.* The noun we always think of as a verb.

Shyness, *n.* Conceit that just can't find the words.

Small talk, *n.* A compulsive game of word association played by congenially retarded adults.

Striptease, *n.* A buildup too slow for the mind with a finale too fast for the eye.

Television, *n.* Diversion for those with nothing to be diverted from.

Thesis, *n.* An acquired topic in search of an original significance.

Wit, *n.* Flash in the pen.

Apart from its mischievous satisfactions, composing devilish definitions can only help your writing. Best of all, it's piecemeal, fast-take writing, something you can do at various times during the day when you have a free moment. It is an exercise in coming up with clear and forceful sentences, and sentences that pack a little twist or even a wallop at that; in the discipline of finding just the perfect word, that proverbial *mot juste;* and in being brief and to the point. Having a dictionary close by won't hurt. (Dictionary, *n.* A reference book that tells rigidly how words are used loosely.)

Devilish defining is the art of the lexical one-liner.

The deliberately misspelled word in last week's column was *graineries*. It's *granaries*.

THE LIKE-NESS MONSTER

WORD OF THE WEEK: *eye dialect*—words respelled for a dialectal effect

QUOTE OF THE WEEK: "Style is as much under the words as in the words."

—GUSTAVE FLAUBERT

Among the published sentences that have landed in the Wordwizard observational in-tray in recent weeks are these: "I was like seventeen years old." "I mean could you like love me?" "He goes, like, 'We can get into your house.'" "John is like, 'Let's do it.'" "Can you do, like, jackknives?" "She was, like, yelling at me?"

You can see what these sentences have, like, in common?

If you've been living in a bunker, you may be under the impression that *like* is chiefly a preposition meaning "similar to." This is old-fashioned. The word *like* in the U.S. of A. today is being heard mostly as an abbreviation, capable of many meanings—or half-meanings—with a minimum of breath or thought.

The new *like* has become the magic word announcing "I'm flailing verbally and it's easier this way." It's become a kind of psychological punctuation or lingual handrail for the syntactically "cool" (or dysfunctional). A far cry from the old hipster's "Like crazy, man!" it's as hip as a prefrontal lobotomy.

Like sometimes means "for example" ("She would drive to, like, St. Louis") or "about or approximately" ("It's, like, eight feet long"). It can also now be interpreted as meaning "you won't believe this" ("There were, like, six inches of ice on my car roof")—an attention-calling emphasizer, the way "get this" used to be.

But you may be surprised to learn that the neo-*like* can also mean (1) "I hesitate to say the exact words, you know, *correctly* and want to appear modest, cool, and palsy-walsy"; (2) "Vaguely, but I'm probably way off"; (3) "Past tenses are difficult for me—let's get back to the simple present"; (4) "It's kind of exhausting to get the words together"; or (5) "Predicates are tough—I need a breather!"

The new Like-ness Monster falls into the category of a filler or pause word, what linguistic scholars call filled pauses or hesitation forms. As a pathological language condition—the use of *um, er, you know, I mean,* and the like (including now the *like*)—such verbal stammering is known as embolalia. That is, *like* has become a kind of stalling-tactic twitch. The speaker skids to a screeching pause and takes a big mental deep breath before *not* following through with coherent sentence structure. (In the grammatical fault called the run-on sentence, there is sometimes the so-called comma splice, or partial stop when there should be a full one; the new, knee-jerk *like* is a kind of all-purpose splice, but a liason signaling no follow-through.) Unlike the cliché, it seems more preverbal than proverbial.

As uncontrollable as Cher's snaking tongue or the crackling of incessantly chewed bubble gum, the overuse of *like* is approaching a national pathological condition. Is the generation of baby boomers being succeeded by the generation of like mumblers? Like-orrhea (it's not a pretty word, but none other will do) is mindless and/or insecure speech. It's the watchword of Specificity Lassitude: the inability to be clear, on the mark, and complete. It is laziness about having to bother about a simple and complete sentence (clause, really), about putting one's words expressing a thought into some form of rudimentary order, about the elementary syntax of human communication. Note how it's used, and you'll sense that it is also a little flag of insecurity, an "are you with me or against me" thrown in intermittently, repeatedly, drearily, uncontrollably. A four-letter stammer, it says, "Whoa, English is just a little too fast for me." Ironically, then, *like* is the main word for people who don't particularly, like, like good English.

Perhaps I'm too late. Have you already caught the virus?

It wasn't that long ago that most people comfortably used pauses to collect their thoughts or phrasing. They honored the sentence pause, the nice little moment of hesitation or reflection, before resuming—not abandoning—the thought in progress. Some of us still do. But nowadays more and more people "can't deal with" even moments of silence, and whenever there's a flash of verbal uncertainty it's more often than not desperately filled in with an all-purpose *like.* The *like*s often go with the *go*s, or the equally popular use of *go* to mean "speak," "respond," "ask," "act like," "gesture," or "solve Fermat's last theorem," as in "And he goes, like, 'I'm honored to receive the Nobel prize for literature.' " Tune in to some *like*s, and you'll probably be hearing some *go*s. *Go,* too, you might say, has become a going concern.

The news gets worse. This new "meaning" for the word *like* is now countenanced in the dictionary as "used interjectionally in informal speech often to emphasize a word or phrase . . . or for an apologetic, vague, or unassertive effect"; or, when as a conjunction with the verb *be* or with *it's,* to "introduce" or "to report a generally held opinion," respectively. Mind you, we're talking here about utterances like (forgive the old-fashioned use of the word) "She was, like, awesome" and "Joe didn't want to, like, be present" and "And I'm like, What's going on here?" Or should the last example be written, with quotation marks, "And I'm like, 'What's going on here?' "—giving *like* the stature of a verb?

Mr. Wordwizard differs with the dictionary and doesn't even beg to. The only thing the new, all-American, verbally lallygagging *like* "emphasizes" is the speaker's communicational imbecility. The only thing it "introduces" is an admission that one doesn't want to bother completing a grammatical sentence, or maybe can't. And saying that it is used for an apologetic, vague, or unassertive "effect" suggests it is used by articulate people as some intentional, rhetorical device—which is not quite the truth of the matter.

Its epidemic popularity is due partly, I think, to the fact that people think it is a kind of "make nice" modifier to "bond" with others. It reassures them that you, too, are clumsy of speech, that you're not threateningly articulate and coherent. (Linguists call this kind of semantically empty "sharing" language phatic communion. Scholar S. I. Hayakawa saw such words as a "presymbolic form of nuzzling" and called them purr-words.)

In our times, being humbly well-spoken can be construed as being threateningly elitist.

However the dictionary may explain it, today's like-orrhea is a sorry symptom of declining language skills. Curiously, the misuse of the word *like* was a cause célèbre once before, back in the 1950s, when a cigarette manufacturer flaunted the slogan "Winston tastes good like a cigarette should." Defenders of good English were outraged at this baldly, sportily illiterate use of the word as a conjunction. What a trifle this national controversy of forty years ago seems today! Any of those English defenders still around today might want to stuff cigarettes into their ears were they confronted with the new *like* plague now among us.

My inveighing against its mindlessness aside, what is so *wrong* with like-orrhea?

It adds no real meaning, merely signaling the speaker's inability to speak in simple and competent

English sentences, or the need to stall vocally every ten or twenty seconds—or need to sound, like, cool and un-assuming.

Its continual use interrupts otherwise coherent speech to an annoying degree. If using simple tenses and clauses and grammar is one of the joys of speaking English, the *like* crutch is disruptive and takes away the joy. Is grammar so important? Yes, it's so important. English, while it should be natural, honest, and adapt-able, needs a certain degree of good posture.

It detracts from anything of interest otherwise said because its use tells the intelligent listener that the speaker may not be worth listening to.

It has become so prevalent and unconscious as to be a kind of speech impediment of a whole generation— maybe two generations.

If it spreads (other than in dialogue) into written En-glish, set off in each instance by commas, you may be seeing more commas than you ever wanted to see.

It suggests that—a lot more young people today are sexually active than grammatically active?

To highlight exactly what like-orrhea hath wrought or brought upon our English language, let us quote, by way of contrast, a small passage from the great English nov-elist Jane Austen:

"She was a woman rather of sound than of quick abil-ities, whose difficulties in coming to any decision in this instance were great, from the opposition of two leading principles. She was of strict integrity herself, with a deli-cate sense of honour; but she was as desirous of saving Sir Walter's feelings, as solicitous for the credit of the family, as aristocratic in her ideas of what was due to them, as anybody of sense and honesty could well be. She was a benevolent, charitable, good woman, and ca-pable of strong attachments; most correct in her con-duct, strict in her notions of decorum, and with manners that were held a standard of good breeding. She had a cultivated mind, and was, generally speaking, rational and consistent—but she had prejudices on the side of ancestry; she had a value for rank and consequence, which blinded her a little to the faults of those who possessed them."

Now let us imagine Ms. Austen's cogent lines written in contemporary like-orrhea:

"She was, like, a woman rather of sound than of quick abilities, whose, like, difficulties in coming to any decision in this instance were, like great, from the opposition of two leading principles. Like, she was of, like strict integrity herself, with, like, a delicate sense of honour . . ."

Need we, like, go on here?

What is the cure for like-orrhea?

The great English writer George Orwell, still admired today for his concern about clarity and truth in language, did not favor the particularly British mannerism of using *not un-* locutions, with a kind of snobbish coyness, as in "It's not uninteresting" instead of, plainly, "It's interesting." Orwell had a solution. "One can cure oneself of the *not un-* formation by memorizing this sentence: 'A not unblack dog was chasing a not unsmall rabbit across a not ungreen field.' "

I suggest either of two ways to cure yourself of like-orrhea.

One is to make a resolution that every time you catch yourself using the new all-purpose *like* in a sentence, stop—and punish yourself by repeating that sentence but substituting for each *like* the word *kumquat.*

The other cure is to memorize this sentence, which incorporates more traditional and valid phrases using *like:*

Like, like as not, like Jane had no, like, liking for the, like, likes of, like, Dick, like it or not.

The deliberately misspelled word in last week's column was *dessicated.* It's *desiccated.*

Latin to Go

WORD OF THE WEEK: *baragouin*—unintelligible speech

QUOTE OF THE WEEK: "The adjective is the banana peel of the parts of speech."

—CLIFTON FADIMAN

English is rich, but Latin is quick.

Word-saving—or economizing on the number of syllables you have to use in saying something—always has its virtues. And at times it's worth borrowing from another language to be brief.

For example, can you think of a way in English to say "Why does there have to be all this verbiage?" or "Please, do you have to go on and on?" or "Why must you be so long-winded?" using only two short words, only three syllables?

Would you consider Latin?

You know, that dead language they used to teach a lot of in grammar schools, later just a little of in high school, and today, usually, almost none of from grammar school through graduate school. Yet that so-called dead language is very much a living part of many of the English words you speak today. Linguistically and culturally, Latin is part of your *roots*.

If you're willing to have people mistake you for being the learned type, you can express any variety of the above question with a catchy Romanism: *Quid multa?* It may be Latin, but isn't it easy? Why say, "Why such a long song and dance about this?" when you can stop the flow with three syllables: *Quid multa?*

Because they've dropped Latin from primary and secondary education doesn't mean you might not enjoy dropping a little Latin—and saving on words—in your everyday conversation.

Why learn some useful Latin phrases? First, they'll impress the heck out of your friends (even if they say "What?" and you have to, noblesse oblige, translate). Not even most college professors today can coolly drop words from an ancient tongue. Second, the kind of easy Latin expressions I'll mention here are not only brief, they're kind of *catchy*. Third, learning a little classic-speak could improve your understanding of English and its Latin roots and, who knows, maybe even interest you in learning Latin, not a bad thing.

And fourth, if you've had a half-decent education and at least read newspapers, you've been speaking broken Latin all your life.

What Latin have you been speaking? Such phrases as *vice versa, et cetera, verbatim, tempus fugit, sui generis, ipso facto, ad hoc, status quo, sine qua non, sic transit gloria mundi, rigor mortis, pro tempore, prima facie, post mortem, per se, persona non grata, per diem, non compos mentis, ne plus ultra, mutatis mutandis, modus operandi, modus vivendi, memento mori, magna cum laude, mirabile dictu, mea culpa, lapsus linguae, in medias res, inabsentia, habeas corpus, flagrante delicto, de gustibus non est disputandum, carpe diem, ad lib(itum), quid pro quo, Q.E.D., ad hominem, in loco parentis, sanctum sanctorum.* . . . Come on, at least some of these?

Even most well-educated people feel a little bad that they don't know a little more about the classical languages. Erudite writers and scholars sometimes use Latin quotations, but most of those lines from the toga-and-pomegranite days of Cicero, Catullus, and Horace appear lengthy and difficult in these modern times.

But if you think Latin—that stuff from churches and tombstones and lawyers—is always dry as dust, you're Classically wrong. Some Latin phrases are like little jingles and not at all that hard to remember. They're short and, if not alliterative or rhyming, have a crisp ring to them. This is not surprising, since Latin was, is, a compact and pithy tongue, free of articles and many of the little words, or particles, that can dilute or clutter up English.

To broaden your verbal horizons, here are a few Latin gems for your consideration. I've chosen them to whet your appetite. But they're just appetizers, not intimidating entrees. The idea here is that they're useful because in most cases, they're briefer than their counterpart expressions in English would be. They're handily holophrastic: They say a lot in a little. No state mottoes or legalese here, just some Classic grace notes to salt, or pepper, your conversation.

If you don't like losing, there's *Vae victis!*—"Woe to (or alas for) the vanquished!"

When somebody accuses you of something he or she is guilty of, you can say "You, too." Or for variety, *Tu quoque.*

Similarly, we often say "God forbid." Why not, for a change, *Absit omen*? Likewise, instead of saying "No offense (intended)," you can say *Absit invidia.*

We're all familiar with the thought that one can or should learn from painful experiences. To make your point about this in conversation, you can say, "You know, bad as things can be, you always nonetheless learn something from it." Or you can say more succinctly, with a touch of rhyme, *Quae nocent docent,* "Things that hurt us teach us." ("No pain, no gain" doesn't mean quite the same thing.)

If you do something on a simple whim or impulse or of your own accord, you're doing it *ex mero motu.*

Heated discussions and cold arguments always remind us that human beings don't seem to have been born to agree about things. *Quot homines, tot sententiae* says it all: "There are as many viewpoints as there are people." (This is not to be confused with "So many women, so little time" or its gender counterpart.) A parallel maxim regarding the dangers of being too rich is *Quot servi, tot hostes,* or "So many servants, so many enemies." If an argument is won and there is nothing more to talk about, there is *Cadit quaestio,* "the question falls."

If you want to chastize somebody that not knowing the law is no excuse, you might as well sound authoritatively like a lawyer: *Ignoratia legis neminem excusat.*

Do you appreciate that person who is immediately generous, who offers help or funds with no persuading? You can think or refer to that donor with *Bis dat qui cito dat,* "He gives twice who gives promptly."

Then there are all those guilty parties, politicians and the like, who say nothing or try the silent treatment when confronted with their misdeeds. You can sum them up in three little words: *Cum tacent, clamant,* "While they are silent, they speak out"—or their silence is an admission. Then again, *Mundus vult decipi,* or "The world wants to be deceived."

How is *Nunc pro tunc* for a catchy bit of Latin? Meaning "now for then," it refers to any action or decision that has a retroactive effect, that is to be applied back then.

The value of teaching for learning oneself is something many teachers will vouch for, and they can sum it up with a Latin spin. *Doce ut discas* is "Teach so that you can learn," and *Qui docet, discit* is "The one who teaches others learns himself." There's also *Docendo discimus,* "We learn by teaching." Yet another variation on this theme allows you to throw in the word *disco: Docendo disco,* "I learn by teaching others."

The Romans seemed to appreciate the value of experience as well. Among the catchphrases they've passed down to us are *Experientia docet stultos,* "Experience teaches even fools." A little more cautionary is the thought that the way you live determines the way you die or, more compactly, *Qualis vita, finis ita.* This may be another way of saying, "Be wisely moderate," or *Ne quid nimis.* "Hunger teaches many lessons" is *Multa docet fames.* A little more optimistic is the sentiment that all things are to the good, or *Omnia bona bonis.* If the thought you want to get across is to trust a person who has tried or to believe the person who has had experience, you can save words with *Experto crede.* Similarly, there's "The beaten (or used) path is the safe path," or *Via trita, via tota.* If it's too late to pull your chestnuts out of the fire, *Jacta est alea* says "The die is cast." If you want to help another but are in no position to, a nice apology is *Volo, non valeo,* "I am willing but unable."

Latin also offers counterparts to common English adages. In Latin, "Like father, like son" is *Mala gallina, malum ovum,* or "Bad hen, bad egg." "Look before you leap" is *Respice finem.* "First come, first served" is *Potior est qui prior est.* And how about "There must be a woman behind it," or "Cherchez la femme"? The Classic version is *Dux femina facti.*

Another instance where Latin offers more than one epigram concerns the importance of giving love. The Latin for "To win love, show love to others" is the nicely simple *Ut amoris, ama.* Or if you prefer, "Love begets love," *Amor gignit amorem.* To show a generous spirit say, *Detur digniori,* "Let it be given to the most deserving."

But not all in life is love. If you want to advise someone who is not treating you too well that "I return tit for tat," advise them *Par pari refero.* Or nicely brief for a vow to get back at someone next time, there's *Cras mihi,* "My turn tomorrow."

If your antipathy is directed not at people but at the hunger for celebrity gossip in American media today, this does the job nicely: *Increduli odimur,* "We don't believe it and can't stand the subject."

Euphony is the word for what is pleasant to say or

hear. *Ubi mel, ibi apes* has such a nice ring about it that you might not care what it means, but, still, you should. It's "Where there is honey, there are bees." No explanation needed.

Whether it's English or Latin, remember *Sermo index animo,* or "Speech is an index of the mind"; or *Verba sunt indices animi,* "Words are indices of the mind." Meanwhile, *Age quod agis,* "Do what you are doing" (or "Just attend to the business at hand").

Please don't have a nice day. Rather, *Vive, vale.* Farewell and be happy.

The deliberately misspelled word from last week's column was *liason.* It's *liaison.*

BODY LANGUAGE

WORD OF THE WEEK: *ipse dixit*—an unsupported assertion or statement

QUOTE OF THE WEEK: "I suppose some editors are failed writers—but so are most writers."

—T. S. ELIOT

Up for playing doctor—linguistically? At least about some of the more basic, close-to-home physical things of day-to-day life?

Like the furfur on your friend's shoulder, the spiloma your sister is proud of, the cutis anserina that scary movie gave you?

Most medical terminology is something we'd rather leave to the doctors. We don't particularly want to relate clinical polysyllables to our afflictions—all those pathology terms ending in *-itis, -osis, -ia, -oma,* and *-esia,* all those procedures ending in *-oscopy, -ectomy, -plasty,* and *-otomy.* Those of us who are not physicians have medicine chests full enough of prescription English—all those brand-name medications ending in *-ex, -in,* or *-ine, -ol* or *-al, -ac. . . .*

But there's no harm in swelling your other chest (not the medicine one) with some interesting words closer to home medically than the hospital: legitimate but rather unfamiliar, formaldahyde-smelling terms for commonplace physical symptoms or processes that we're all familiar with in our everyday lives. They're names for bodily traits or ailments, that is, but not the household words we use. They're medical terms (some of them older medical terms) but not that medical—most will be found in a general unabridged dictionary.

Some iatric (medical) words, that is, are interesting because they refer not to standard illnesses but to things even more familiar to us—as when we look in the mirror each day.

If I run them by you in a little scene-setting (no action) skit, how many can you guess the meanings of?

Imagine two Verona High School teenagers, Romeo and Juliet, before their first date. At their homes they're getting dressed before their first evening out together. Imagine them thinking, as only teenagers can, about their physical appearance:

Clean as a whistle and free of bromhidrosis, Romeo brushed his teeth savagely until he winced. He had a flaming parulis, and it hurt. Not as bad, at least, as the aposteme he had had two months before. Where was that powder for his tinea cruris? At least the tinea pedia was gone. He peered closely into the mirror over the sink for any new whelks, which were so annoying—if not as bad as the furuncle his uncle had. His uncle also had alopecia, which he, Romeo, hoped he'd never get.

With his washcloth, Romeo checked for cerumen, then moved the right side of his face closer to the mirror. The hordeolum was still there. He couldn't stop thinking of Juliet, who was getting over a coryza and some erythema caloricum on her pretty shoulders when he had met her last week. Would he get to kiss that sexy nevus of hers tonight? The thrill of that very thought of her gave him a globus hystericus. Darn, there was a grume on his neck from shaving! Would he get lucky and tomorrow have instead some osculatory hematomas there?

Romeo couldn't help being a bit nervous before any first date. There were his occasional blepharisms or, in movie theaters, tingling obdormition if he didn't keep recrossing his legs. In a theater with another girl once, he got a sudden intramuscular cramp and cried out to his and everybody else's embarrassment.

Meanwhile, inspecting an agnail and some schizotrichia, Juliet was thinking of Romeo's cute ephelides. If only she had some! But she did have a spiloma that her girlfriends would die for, and for the moment no embarrassing bubukles or big stand-up comedos.

Romeo was the jock type, which she liked. When she first saw him on the football practice field he had several ecchymoses, even a slight circumorbital hematoma and an epistaxis. Juliet wasn't exactly a jock, but she had keratomas from jogging and was just getting over a talar stremma. Also, a sore bleb from using the iron, which would probably, rats, become an eschar.

More of a worry was the singultus. Every first date ended up with embarrassing singultus. Nervousness. Why did some girls get singultus, some guys diaphoresis? She still had a slight tussis and would need a hankie for her rhinorrhea. But a date with Romeo—it was enough to give any girl cutis anserina! And if things didn't go well—how could they not with Romeo!—she could always plead a cephalalgia and go home early.

Translation time. A comparison reading of the following passage with the one above will tell you the meanings of those forbidding medical terms:

Clean as a whistle and free of foul-smelling sweat, Romeo brushed his teeth savagely until he winced. He had a flaming gumboil, and it hurt. Not as bad, at least, as the abscess he had had two months before. Where was that powder for his jock itch? At least the athlete's foot was gone. He peered closely into the mirror over the sink for any new pimples, which were so annoying— if not as bad as the boil his uncle had had. His uncle was also bald, which he, Romeo, hoped he'd never be.

With his washcloth, Romeo checked for ear wax, then

moved the right side of his face closer to the mirror. The eyelid stye was still there. He couldn't stop thinking of Juliet, who was getting over a head cold and some sunburn on her pretty shoulders when he had met her last week. Would he get to kiss that sexy mole of hers tonight? The thrill of that very thought of her gave him a lump in his throat. Darn, there was a clot of blood on his neck from shaving! Would he get lucky and tomorrow have instead some hickeys there?

Romeo couldn't help being a bit nervous before any first date. There were his occasional eyelid twitches or, in movie theaters, his foot falling asleep if he didn't keep recrossing his legs. In a theater with another girl once, he got a sudden charley horse and cried out to his and everybody else's embarrassment.

Meanwhile, inspecting a hangnail and some split ends, Juliet was thinking of Romeo's cute freckles. If only she had some! But she did have a birthmark that her girlfriends would die for, and for the moment no embarrassing pimples or big stand-up blackheads.

Romeo was the jock type, which she liked. When she first saw him on the football practice field he had several black-and-blue marks, even a slight black eye and a nosebleed. Juliet wasn't exactly a jock, but she had calluses from jogging and was just getting over a sprained ankle. Also, a sore blister from using the iron, which would probably, rats, become a burn scab.

More of a worry was hiccups. Every first date ended up with embarrassing hiccups. Nervousness. Why did some girls get hiccups, some guys profuse sweating? She still had a slight cough and would need a hankie for her runny nose. But a date with Romeo—it was enough to give any girl goose bumps! And if things didn't go well— how could they not with Romeo!—she could always plead a headache and go home early.

The deliberately misspelled word from last week's column was *pomegranite*. It's *pomegranate*.

DON'T GIVE ME
ANY XXXX

WORD OF THE WEEK: *glottogonic*—pertaining to the origins of language

QUOTE OF THE WEEK: "The ear is the only true writer and the only true reader."

—ROBERT FROST

How do you clean up foul language? With other language.

Did you know that *sir-reverence* once had a dirty meaning?

Are you up to some quaint down-and-dirty talk? Or rather, to some curious old words that people who overuse a certain four-letter word might consider using instead, to give us all a break?

I know—I've already columned-out against that other trendy obscenity that I called the *a*-word. But American swearing is becoming awfully tiresome, and it's time to offer sayable alternatives (much preferable to viable alternatives) to another endemic four-letter word.

The four-letter word, the *s*-word, is that one meaning excrement. As a noun, it goes back to 1585. Have no fear, it's not going to be spelled out here. It's tiresome enough hearing it uttered and re-uttered, as a throw-away cuss, everywhere today. It's become iniquitously ubiquitous. It's used in various insult phrases; as a throw-in word, for just about anything, to give a sentence a note of anger or contempt; and of course, by itself, as a useful exclamation to let off steam.

You don't need to be told that this shushlike expletive is sadly overused today. It's perhaps America's favorite one-word outburst.

As in: "You're full of xxxx," "Don't give me any xxxx," "xxxx!" "You miserable little xxxx," "No xxxx!" "That's a crock of xxxx," "I'm scared xxxx-less," "Xxxx or get off the pot," "I almost xxxx a brick," "It isn't worth xxxx," "We're up xxxx creek," "We're in deep xxxx," and "Xxxx, man!" (Here we're using, instead of blank spaces, some quadruple x's. The other standard printer's way to render obscenity without spelling it out is with miscellaneous symbol and punctuational characters—or dingbatted maledicta, as scatological scholar Reinhold Aman calls *!+%!?!)

The English language has numerous interestingly specific terms for the droppings of particular animals. For example, otter dung is *spraints,* fox or badger dung is *feance,* hare dung is *crottels,* deer dung is *fewmets,* and badger dung is *werdrobe.* (An obsolete general word for manure is *laetation.*) But in the human domain, there seems to be little imagination for anything but that *s*-word.

Since xxxx seems to be so much on everybody's speech, we might as well acquaint ourselves with some curious old words having the same meaning. Instead of being stiffly censorious, why not just try to open up the verbal field to some fair competition—some old-fashioned synonyms that might make for a little variety in foul talk? Instead of name droppings, droppings names?

Scatology is the realm I'm stepping around here. *Scatology* has two meanings: the serious study of excrement, as by a zoologist willing to get his hands dirty, or the "field" of droppings, if you will; and obscenity as a literary genre or a personal interest. Heck with biology or obscenity, let's just unearth a few little-known synonyms for that word that has become our favorite pungent metaphor. How many, besides *feces, dung, manure, or-*

dure, stool, compost, and a few more obvious ones, do you know for that tiresome quadriliteralism? (*Quadriliteralism* is a fifteen-letter word for that four-letter word.) The only proper synonyms for urine I'm aware of are *miction* and *emiction.*

Yes, unavoidably, impassibly, this is a whole Wordwizard column about increment, or enlarging your horizons. Among curious old synonyms for the four-x word you'll turn up during a stroll down dictionary lane (the *Oxford English Dictionary)* are the following:

Scumber is an old word for excrement, its earliest citation in the OED being 1400. Originally applied to the droppings of dogs or foxes, it came to be used jocularly of human droppings.

If you know some foul French, you'll know *merd.* But you may not know that it dropped into English usage as far back as 1477, with its meaning not at all cleaned up. The OED also has the adjectival *merdous.*

A fifteenth-century word for xxxx was *stercory* (1495). If you look in *Webster's Third New International Dictionary,* you'll also find the archaic word *stercorary,* which refers to a kind of weather-proof storage pit for manure; *stercoration,* "the act of dressing with manure" (presumably not dressing in a sartorial sense); and, referring to insects, *stercoricolous,* "living in dung," and *stercovorous* or *stercoral,* "dung-eating" (or scatophagous).

Two sixteenth-century words for ordure are *ejestion* (1547) and *sir-reverence* (1592 in this sense). As can be seen in Shakespeare, *sir-reverence* was also a term of careful apology thrown in before saying something that might have been thought to be presumptuous, offensive, or pushy. Talk about double duty for a word! How many other terms do you know that can mean both "if I may be so bold as to venture to say" and "feces"? Certainly not xxxx.

In the seventeenth century, the word *tantadlin* (1654), or *tantoblin,* originally referred to a pastry or tart, but sure enough, those with a slangy imagination got hold of it, and it was soon being used to refer to a different kind of little pie (to be daringly specific, a turd). There was also the word *dejection* (1605), or sometimes *dejections,* used in its literal Latin sense of something "thrown down."

Three more words for human waste matter came into usage in the eighteenth century, *eccrisis* (1706), *dejecture* (1731), and *feculence* (1733 in this sense). *Excreta* dates back in writing to 1857, and related to it today we have *excretion* and *excretions.*

Sometimes two words are preferred to one in English for sensitive matters, and one term that came into use in the eighteenth century for excrement was *alvine dejections.* The word *alvine* meant "abdominal."

Surely the two most appealing terms of all these are *sir-reverence* and *alvine dejections.* If only as a relief from that overused four-letter word, couldn't we use them today?

I hope this column hasn't been a complete waste.

The deliberately misspelled word in last week's column was *formaldahyde.* It's *formaldehyde.*

ZOUNDS ALLY KINGLISH

WORD OF THE WEEK: *concettism*—literary use of conceits or erudite allusions

QUOTE OF THE WEEK: "Our language, one of our most precious natural resources, deserves at least as much protection as our woodlands, streams and whooping cranes."

—JAMES LIPTON

Talking—or reading aloud—to oneself has its merits. You know that somebody, at least, is listening, and it's sometimes just a way to let off steam or perform for yourself. But it can also help you to appreciate certain strange pieces of writing, like:

"Wants pawn term dare worsted ladle gull hoe life wetter murder inner ladle cordage honor itch ofer lodge, dock, florist. Disk ladle gull orphan worry putty ladle rat cluck wetter ladle rat hut, an fur disk raisin pimple colder Ladle Rat Rotten Hut."

If you could decipher the meaning of these two sentences, chances are you did it by talking aloud a bit, by moving your lips. Or put another way, by reading with your ears.

Language, as we know, can be in spoken or written form. Interestingly enough, a certain kind of English, made up of quite legitimate words, is total nonsense when seen in print but understandable when uttered.

What in the world kind of English is that? It's Zounds Ally Kinglish (or sounds-alike English), or homophonic wordplay. It's more than fun, because you can use it as a kind of code to write in (to a friend, ally, or lover, of course).

The title of this column probably puzzled you when you first saw it. The key to understanding its real meaning lies in hearing the words pronounced. With nobody else around, that means you. ("Read your own lips," somebody might say.) To comprehend—or compose—this wondrous kind of English, you have to be willing to talk to yourself. Mutter or whisper, at least.

The strange words above—strange only in their assortment and seeming meaninglessness as a whole—are the first paragraph of "Ladle Rat Rotten Hut," a piece by Howard Chace that, the authors of the school anthology *About Language* tell us, "has long circulated through English departments."

"Wan moaning," Chace's tale continues, "Ladle Rat Rotten Hut's murder colder inset, 'Ladle Rat Rotten Hut, heresy ladle basking winsome burden barter an shirker cockles. Tick disk ladle basking tutor cordage offer groin-murder hoe lifts honor udder site offer florist. Shaker lake! Dun stopper laundry wrote! Dun stopper pekc floors! Dun daily-doily inner florist, an yonder nor sorghum stenches, dun stopper torque wet strainers!' "

No translations here. The fun should be all yours. Not that it's all that easy, and if you can breeze through all of Chace's sentences without getting stuck here and there, you may have a genius for Zounds Ally Kinglish. If you become a fluent reader, so to speak, you won't even have to talk to yourself, maybe not even move your lips. You'll be able to make the necessary adjustments mentally, silently.

Zounds Ally Kinglish is an enchanting phonic phenomenon in English (or other language). It consists in rendering phrases or sentences of conventional English in other words (literally). It's a tricky business. You're dealing with something visual, words in print, but what's really going on is auditory, words as we know them to be pronounced. As a bizarre wordplay medium, it works only because we all have a basic sense of how words, or syllables, usually sound when uttered.

Traces of this phenomenon can be seen in homophonic mispellings, like *pole* for *poll* or *wear* for *ware*. These are sometimes called homonym slips. They result in such sentences as *It was a hare's breadth escape* and *He was just taking her for granite*.

Professor John Bremner of the University of Kansas has called this "sonic writing." William Safire calls mistaken interpretations of heard speech "mondegreens," a term (coined, he says, by Sylvia Wright) derived from mishearing the line from a Scottish ballad "And laid him on the green" as "And Lady Mondegreen." The mishearing of English by foreign-born people and red-blooded Americans alike yields wondrous sentences, wondrous because they're often not merely defective English but very amusingly defective English. They're sort of malapropisms inside out. For example, a New York City newspaper some years ago reported how various young children had mistaken notions of the words to "The Star-Spangled Banner," which they had sung but never seen in print. One boy believed our national anthem began, "José, can you see . . ."

As you can see, Zounds Ally Kinglish also involves approximations of sounds but uses them to create a kind of parallel language. In essence it's a simple challenge: to *sound* the same thing in different words. It's a kind of game that's been passed down over the years. Yet more clever, it's been used to render English in pseudo-French in a charming little book by Luis d'Antin van Rooten, *Mots d'Heures: Gousse, Rames*. Homophones have also been used humorously to represent the sporty diphthongal Australian accent, or Strine ("Australian"). Strine was evidently created by a man named Afferbeck Lauder in his 1965 book *Let Stalk Strine*. Lauder also made pronunciational sport of the affected West End accent of London by transliterating it to Fraffly, as in

"Fraffly caned a few" ("Frightfully kind of you"), in a 1968 book, *Fraffly Well Spoken.*

But different-word English is challenging fun enough without mixing in a foreign language. To be able to pick the best alternative words that will reproduce an understandable narrative or message when read aloud (or mentally aloud) is a fascinating exercise. How close can you get to the sound of the real words?

The delight of the overall effect is the conjunction of the visual with the aural, of the look of a skein of non-sensical words with the blossoming of sense when they are read aloud. Written poetry, with its visual form on the page and resultant rhythms and emphases when read aloud, is similar, perhaps, in being a kind of creative counterpoint.

Which will be the best words, the closest words for one's rewording? Actually, the real challenge is to use words *not* precisely homophonic (for example, not *reed* for *read)* but still make the result understandable.

There may be several or only limited possibilities. In "Ladle Rat Rotten Hut," Howard Chace renders "Once upon a time there was a little girl who lived with her mother in a cottage on the edge of a large, dark forest" as "Wants pawn term dare worsted ladle gull hoe lift wetter murder inner ladle cordage honor itch offer lodge, duck, florist."

Chace could also have given us, "Wan step on it I'm th'air Warsaw lid dull gore ill olive twit Herm other in-let . . . ?"

It's not so easy, no?

The charm of this unique smorgasboard of wordplay is that the matching of sounds is never quite perfect. It's always a little off, or more than a little off, and the halting dialectal effect can only make you smile. Zounds Ally Kinglish, in other words, comes off as a special kind of dialectal humor.

If you become a practiced composer of Zounds Ally Kinglish, you'll have a challenging verbal game to play for life. It requires no board or deck of cards, only a pencil and paper and perhaps (optional) a dictionary.

You'll increase your awareness of English pronunciation.

You'll expand your vocabulary—you'll have to come up with some unexpected words now and then. You'll find new meaning in the phrase *in other words*.

You'll also have an entertaining code for your diary or for notes or love letters to those special people who, like you, can read with their ears.

That is, yule all Soave anent ordain ink coed furrier diarrhea fur Notzer lava let tours tooth owes spacial peep hole hula eye queue kin rid wither rears.

The deliberately misspelled word in last week's column was *impassibly*. It's (in the sense of not passable) *impassably*.

CONVERSATION JAW-OPENERS

WORD OF THE WEEK: *synonymy*—a comparison or elucidation of synonyms

QUOTE OF THE WEEK: "Plain English—everybody loves it, demands it—from the other fellow."

—JACQUES BARZUN

If unusual, baffling words can ever have some practical use, it might be as provocative icebreakers of the non-nautical kind.

You can sometimes get an initial conversation going at the drop of a word—an unusual word—or two. As in, *For quiescence, give me the vacivity of a finitor.*

Who can ignore a calmly delivered bit of legitimate incomprehensibility like that? Once you've got the conversation started, you can take it from there with your tried and true English. But the age-old problem has always been coming up with the conversation-opener, the icebreaker, particularly when trying to get to know a member of the opposite sex.

There's always psilology, or vacuous, trivial talk. You can of course stay with the customary tiresome banalities: *Haven't we met before? Awful weather, isn't it? Do you come here often? Nice party, isn't it? What's your sign? How do you know* (name of the host or hostess)? *Hi.* Or you can say something witty.

But what if you're not particularly witty and don't have that ad hoc, ad lib gift in social intercourse?

Try being provocative. Try being lexiphanic.

Lexiphanicism is pretentious or bombastic phraseology. It's using big words, which most commonly means rare Latinate English words. (Etymologically, the word refers to a grandiose speaker in a dialogue, *Lexiphanes,* by Lucian, a Greek satirist of the second century.) If you use unfamiliar words in the academic world to flummox and impress, you're an obscurantist. If you use them for tweedy professorial humor, you're being jocose. But if you use them to get a reaction when you're meeting someone, you're building bridges, being seriously unserious (or is it unseriously serious), and having a little fun. You're helping to increase your interlocutor's vocabulary and elevating the level of usual conversation. An exotic lexiphanicism is less a pick-up line than a pick-it-up line.

To use our above example, in a crowded and noisy atmosphere you can sidle into a conversation with *For peacefulness, give me the emptiness of a horizon.* In fact, you could be not only philosophical but lexiphanic and say, with the same meaning, *For quiescence, give me the vacivity of a finitor.*

Lexiphanic socializing can be assinine or badly done, of course. It is a matter of degree and timing and touch. Such a highfalutin one-liner should be delivered conspiratorially, maybe with a little wink or an arch of the eyebrow (this is highbrow stuff). Or straightfaced, deadpan? Your call.

So here—my secret motive is as always to get readers of this column to get more closely acquainted with a dictionary—are some conversation-stopping conversation-openers. Or closers: not all of them are friendly.

It sticks out all over—you have mancinism. (It sticks out all over—you're left-handed.)
Would you say you're euonymous? (Would you say you're aptly named?)

Is marcidity eudaemonical? (Will thinness make one happy?)

I'm here as a student of psycho-asthenics and agnoiology. (I'm here doing a study of mental deficiency and the necessity of human ignorance.)

Do you find me inficete? (Do you find me dull and humorless?)

I do februations, particularly of peristrephic heads. (I do exorcisms, particularly those of heads that rotate.)

A bad wine is insenescible, do you agree? (A bad wine will never grow old, do you agree?)

What's your favorite lectual lettrure? (What's your favorite bedtime reading?)

Are you oculogyric? (Can you rotate your eyeballs?)

Do you believe in estellation? (Do you believe in astrology?)

Do you believe in arbitrament? (Do you believe in free will?)

You're a cynosure for lippitude. (You're a sight for sore eyes.)

I do make sort of a quillet between an amorous illapse and outright stupration. (I do make sort of a fine distinction between a gradual come-on and outright rape.)

Is it true that male bienseance is in desuetude? (Is it true that chivalry's no longer in fashion?)

I'm a noctivagant sybarite (or *Cyrenaic*). (I'm a nightwandering pleasure-seeker.)

You make me tentigenous. (You turn me on.)

Might I be your banneret in coruscating mail? (Might I be your knight in shining armor?)

May I see your purlicue? (May I see your thumb-to-forefinger line?)

I'm motatorious, and you? (I'm always on the go, and you?)

Please excuse my spawling. (Please excuse my throat-clearing.)

I bet you thought I was ecdemic. (I bet you thought I was foreign.)

I'm amadelphous and eager to contesserate. (I'm gregarious and eager to make friends.)

I note the witzelsucht of your salutation. (I note that you greet me with strained humor.)

I'm a little embarrassed by these cicatrices from my budgerigar. (I'm a little embarrassed by these scars from my parakeet.)

Was my plangent ructation an evagation? (Was my resounding burp a departure from etiquette?)

How do you feel about consenescence? (How do you feel about growing old together?)

It's advesperating. (It's getting late.)

I'm a ragmatical and arreptititious guy. (I'm a wild and crazy guy.)

I'm looking for a proxysm that's synallagmatic. (I'm looking for a close relationship with mutual commitment.)

How about a sabatine dinner and a domenical breakfast? (How about dinner Saturday and breakfast Sunday?)

My velleities regarding you are quite hontous. (My vague wishes regarding you are quite shameful.)

What an adlubescence! (What a delight to meet you.)

Be pedetentous. (Take it careful and slow.)

Let's have a compotation sometime. (Let's have a drink together sometime.)

Are you onymous? (Do you have a name?)

I notice you turn cinereous whenever I give you my salos. (I notice you turn ashen whenever I greet you.)

You have jucundity today, too, replete with such jejune vacuities. (You have a nice day, too, replete with such insipid clichés.)

Do you have a hypokoristikon? (Do you have a pet name?)

Another nippitate, please. (Another ale, please.)

I'm thinking of making a career change from putanism to heredipety. (I'm thinking of making a career change from prostitution to legacy-hunting.)

I'm strictly an aquabib, can't handle ardent spirits. (I'm strictly a water-drinker, can't handle strong liquor.)

Is my outrecuidance that exoteric? (Is my excessive opinion of myself that obvious?)

A ptochocracy is what those jeunesse dorée need. (Rule by the poor is what those yuppies need.)

Do they sell any kind of aosmic usquebaugh here? (Do they sell any kind of odorless whiskey here?)

Are you always so egregiously adient in an epithumetic way? (Do you always come on so strong?)

Your declinature will be trophonian for me. (Your rejection will make me forever sad.)

This column has been brought to you as a public socializing service.

The deliberately misspelled word in last week's column was *smorgasboard.* It's *smorgasbord.*

LOOPY LITERALS

WORD OF THE WEEK: *mid-Atlantic*—mixing British and American accents

QUOTE OF THE WEEK: "Writing is like getting married. One should never commit oneself until one is amazed at one's luck."

—IRIS MURDOCH

"To the letter" is how we carry out things when we're being very correct.

Indeed, the importance of a single alphabetic letter—or its proper position in a word—can't really be exaggerated. A mistaken, misplaced, or missing letter can yield more than a misspelling. It can be an adventure in inadvertent meaning.

Enough writers, famous and not so, have sung the importance of the single word, the just-right word or so-called *mot juste*. It was Mark Twain who reminded us that the difference between the right word and the almost-right word is only the difference between lightning and a lightning bug.

But even lexicographers and authors of word books have very little to say about the phenomenon of the not-just-right letter, or misprint. The difference between the right letter and the almost-right letter is only the difference between lightning and lighting. Or lightening. Or tightening. Or between a bug, a bag, and a bog, which might beg to be big.

Mathematical misprints can have grave consequences. But they don't give us the same wondrous effects as a misprinted letter. A wrong number or a number out of place is just that: a wrong number or a number out of place. Whereas a wrong letter or letter out of place can arch the eyebrow, tickle the fancy, or generate a smile.

If we include not just wrong letters but mistaken shiftings or doublings or omissions of letters, the possibilities go well beyond dull spelling errors. A mere one-twenty-sixth-of-the-alphabet goof, a mere hair to the right or left, so to speak, and you've got the difference between martial aid and marital aid, cofounding a society and confounding a society, the great American novel and the great American navel, a causal relationship and a casual relationship, a man who likes to borrow and a man who likes to burrow, a teacher who aims to inculcate and a teacher who aims to inoculate, a mortal enemy and a mortal enema, a cress at the salad bar and a caress at the salad bar, an editorial caret and an editorial crate, a report based on fact and a report biased on fact, a writing desk and a writhing desk. It's the difference between solider and soldier, expensive and expansive, war bond and Ward Bond, swear and sewer, orotund and rotund, antidote and antivote, exotic and erotic, disparate and desperate, cutlass and cut glass, dress and duress, trap and tarp, palatial and palatal, zany and any.

Printing has been called movable type. It's indeed the movable aspect that can lead to orthographic serendipities. To our eternal reading entertainment, that seemingly infinitessimal single letter can be the difference between a disparately wrong meaning and a desperately wrung meaning.

A slip of the tongue is sometimes called a *lapsus linguae,* but a slip of the pen is a *lapsus calami* (or *lapsus pennae).* Typos, for typographic errors, are what we call happenstance misspellings in print. They're also called literals. Typos are the errors that are not the author's. When noticed, which they usually are, they detract from the text like unmatching buttons on a garment. When writing is doing its job, it engages the reader and time vanishes. But that spell of being engrossed that a reader can feel—one goofy wrong letter can dis-spell it in a moment. More than one or two misprints in an article sends up a Sloppiness flag. Typos are the dandruff of publishing.

Or, to practice what I preach:

Typos rewind us ho munch in English can singe on a tingle litter or the arder of tow latters. Than we usually notice a type indicates out basin familiarity with collect smelling, end al so how the context of wham we're leading tolls us which ward, or spilling, belongs in its peace. Being harp in sporting humbled spillings is being "literal" (or letter-al) in the original tense of that ward. In face, tingle-letter mistakes in print are often called literals. (So much for misspelled sentences. They can be exhausting.)

The more serious the subject, the more outstanding the typo can be. As in the case of religious writing. The common confusion of the words *Calvary* and *cavalry* is a classic example. It's said that the first notable typographical error in the history of printing was *spalm* for *psalm* in a 1457 edition of the Psalter. The printer, Johann Fust, had badly treated Johann Gutenberg, the acknowledged inventor of printing, and some people thought the typographic mistake represented God's wrath. Other early versions of the Bible became known for classic misprints and even named for them. *The Placemaker's Bible* (1562) was so called because of that word appearing in place of *peacemaker*. *The Vinegar Bible* (1717) had "The Parable of the Vinegar" instead of "The Parable of the Vineyard," and *The Murderer's Bible* (1801) had *murderers* instead of *murmurers*.

The English poet A. E. Housman was so demanding about even punctuational accuracy in his poems that he usually refused permission to others to include (and possibly misprint) his poems in anthologies.

Typos (other than errors involving spaces or punctuation) are of two sorts, basically: wrong letters that create nonexistent words, and wrong letters that result in completely different but valid words. It's the second type (no typo for *typo* intended) that can be the most unwitting fun for readers, because it produces inadvertent meanings and often humorously odd sentences. Often the accidental meanings have a kind of fascinating suggestiveness or even truth about them.

Such letter-al shifts have never gone unappreciated, of course. Deliberate wordplay, or rather letterplay, has long been a passion for people fascinated with the effects made possible when word letters are added, deleted, shifted, jumbled, doubled, reversed, or turned upside down. This ingenuity and pranksterism at the purely abecedarian level of the English (or any) language is today called recreational linguistics or logology. Its devotees (who subscribe to the magazine *Word Ways*) have a jargon not only of anagrams, spoonerisms, acrostics, lipograms, and palindromes but also of transposals, antigrams, pangrams, higgledy-piggledies, univocalics, hoity-toities, alternades, hospitable words, charitable words, rhopalics, pair isograms, piano words, typewriter words, and other discovered species of alphabet soup.

Thus, what to other people are mere typographic oddities or errors are to logologists letter changes *(avenue/ avenge)*, letter deletions *(resign/reign)*, letter insertions *(scar/scarf)*, beheadments *(pirate/irate)*, curtailments *(paste/past)*, linkades *(for + reign = foreign)*, metallages *(causal/casual)*, terminal deletions *(magenta/agent)*, and —my favorite—charades *(amiable together/am I able to get her)*. True adepts suspend their normal reading-for-sense for these pursuits and often concoct astonishing epical sentences, lists, and passages.

There are thousands of aficionados who letter in this sport and have a remarkable gift for looking at an innocent single word and seeing possibilities for breeding a whole population of other words out of its letters. It's all a fanatical appreciation of, as verbal juggler Willard

Espy subheads a chapter in one of his books, "slips that pass in the type."

Many otherwise bookish people are no more drawn to this verbal miniaturism than they would be to numerology or rattling and tossing dice from a cup all day. It's a game played at the outer-skin level of language, and even back in the early eighteenth century English essayist and poet Joseph Addison called such preoccupations "false wit." For Addison, basically, true wit had to involve finding resemblance and congruity in ideas (not in manipulating single letters) and be translatable into another language. He also included punning, or "a jingle of words," as a kind of false wit: "I must not here omit, that a famous University of this Land was formerly very much infested with Punns; but whether or no this might not arise from the Fens and Marshes in which it was situated, and which are now drained, I must leave to the Determination of more skilful Naturalists."

Certainly logology is if nothing else a painstaking avocation, but Addison wasn't too appreciative of character-istic wit. "If we must lash one another," he wrote in 1711, "let it be with the manly Strokes of Wit and Satyr; for I am of the old Philosopher's Opinion, That if I must suffer from one or the other, I would rather it should be from the Paw of a Lion, than the Hoof of an Ass. I do not speak this out of any Spirit of Party. There is a most crying Dulness on both Sides. I have seen Tory *Acrosticks* and Whig *Anagrams,* and do not quarrel with either of them, because they are *Whigs* or *Tories,* but because they are *Anagrams* and *Acrosticks.*"

It must be conceded, though, that there's a kind of genius in recreational linguistics. And whether letter-o-mania is a worthy interest or not, there's no question that *accidental* recreational linguistics—or typos—can have its charms.

How better to demonstrate how meaning can turn on a single wrong, missing, extra, or out-of-place letter than to consider some familiar sayings? Let's consider the serendipitous possibilities of meaning with some per-

verted proverbs. (The coining of proverbs is called
paroemiology.) How would familiar saws read if an orthographic saboteur, like me, made a few slight
changes?

Nothing peek, nothing fine.
Loom before you lean.
It never pains but it pouts.
Appeasances are receptive.
Still waiters run deep.
Cesar's wine must be a love suspicion.
A fool and his honey are soon darted.
The leotard cannot change its pots.
Bods will be bods.
Every man has his prince.
Any sort in a store.
Never sneak all of the dead.
Seeing is relieving.
Don't chance houses in midstream.
Faint heart never won fair lay.
You cannot seat your cake and heave it too.
Physician, deal thyself.
Spare the rod and spoil the chill.
Brevity is the soul of wait.
Time lies.
The early bard gets the word.
Nothing dentured, nothing grined.
Haste fakes taste.
Neither a burrower nor a leader be.
A rolling stone rathers no boss.
Discretion is the better tart of palor.
Till gotten, ill pent.
Two is company, three's a rowd.
Dear men sell no talks.
Auctions peak louder than words.
Clothes make the tan.
Practice that you reach.
The eyes are the widow of the foul.
To err is human, to forgive, diving.

Honesty is the bet police.
Her today, on tomorrow.
Moderation in all thinks.
Love is blend.
Time is a great dealer.
Better be sane than worry.
Travel broadens the hind.
Goo things come in mall pickages.
One can't see the fores for the threes.
When the cat's away, the dice will slay.
Don't mount your chickens before they're matched.
The opera isn't over till the fat lad sinks.
All that litters is not old.
The end justifies the beans.
You cannot take a milk pulse out of a cow's ear.
Powder corrupts.
Out of might, out of mind.
Love and let love.
Murmer will out.
Here here's spoke, here's tire.
Where there's a bill, there's a say.
One food urn deserts another.
It takes ale sots to wake a world.
Pact ice make prefect.
Necessity is the bother of invention.
Take ray while the sun shines.
Never say pie.
Beauty is only kin-deep.
Cleanliness is next to bodliness.
Familiarity bleeds contemp.
Crime does now pay.
The spot calls the kennle slack.

The deliberately misspelled word in last week's column was *assinine*. It's *asinine*.

PEDRO CAROLINO AND XENO-ENGLISH

WORD OF THE WEEK: *bos in lingua*—a weighty reason for silence

QUOTE OF THE WEEK: "Words make love with one another."

—ANDRÉ BRETON

Are you at all speaking the xeno-English? What xeno-English is? It is the so charming of mistakes English which be in practice from the un-America born foreignpersons.

Has you to know Pedro Carolino who he is?

If you can understand the above sentences, you then know that xeno-English is my term of choice for not-quite-correct English as used by many well-meaning nonnatives, whether foreigners or recent immigrants. For xeno-English—*xeno* is a combining form meaning "alien" or "strange"—is not just incorrect English. It is enchantingly incorrect English.

Besides the evil that we native speakers do to our own language, there is the nondomestic variety known as pidgin English, a simplified, jargonized English of the Pacific. (A pidgin that has become a region's native language is called a creole.) Derogatorily, the stilted English of people from India has been called babu English.

Xeno-English, however, is jumbled, innocently befuddled English that delights its hearers or readers. It delights because its phrasing and word-mangling are surprising in innocent ways that only a true foreigner could manage. Xeno-English opens up charming possibilities of off-meaning, confounding meaning, double or triple meaning.

The other hallmark of true xeno-English is that it is hard to fake. The opening sentences above are faked, but how many more could be faked before they would look suspiciously fabricated, falsely innocent? You may be very proud of your bad English. But if you're American-born, you can't speak *irresistible* bad English—xeno-English—without great effort. I tried above, but only came up with phony xeno-English.

It's one thing to undo coherent English. It's another to undo it with a magic wand.

Or do you think you could write xeno-English the way the great Pedro Carolino, in his wondrous innocence, could? Who is Pedro Carolino? Read on to learn more about Portugal's gift to extrasensory English syntax.

This column is a tribute to, not a put-down of, barbarized but childlike English. It's usually known as fractured English, but I think the term *xeno-English* is less judgmental, and it should be. A kind of English that brings a smile, not a frown, to the face should not be called broken English. Let no one put a bandage or turniquet on xeno-English.

Besides, Americans commit enough bad English themselves without ridiculing that of foreign-extraction speakers.

All by ourselves we wallow in bad grammar, *like*-orrhea, lazy word slurrings, repetitive obscenities, empty have-a-nice-dayisms, embarrassingly limited vocabularies, simpleton misspellings, all kinds of unspeakably but alas writeably pretentious jargon, and the mindless language inflation (by the advertisers and the media) called hype. Some of us even suffer from xenoglossophilia, or the love of foreign or strange words.

But that doesn't stop us from being amused by the speech of non-Americans. That even includes the British, with some of their peculiar (to us) expressions. England has a long tradition of vociferous abhorrence—or coming down on—Americanisms and what we've "done" to their language. Turnabout is fair play. Why in the world do those Brits say "Oxford play Cambridge" (instead of "plays"), or "She never looked like being suicidal" (instead of "looked as if she were suicidal"), or "They may have done" (instead of just "they may have"), or "It's time to bath the baby" (instead of "bathe")? How can they call a quarter note a crotchet, a dashboard a fascia panel, a sausage a banger? How can they accent *ballet, brochure, valet, café, garage,* and *Maurice* on the first syllable? How can they pronounce *Featherstonehaugh* the way we would "Fanshaw," and *Caius* (College) as we would "keys"? How can they spell that south-of-the-border dish "chilli con carne"?

Never we mind, our subject here is xeno-English and the greatest, most enduring writer of xeno-English the world has ever known, a nineteenth-century Portuguese fellow named Pedro Carolino.

If there is a classic of xeno-English, it is an 1883 phrasebook called (the title itself tells you something is amiss) *New Guide of the Conversation in Portuguese and English.* Its author, one Senhor Pedro Carolino, wanted earnestly to be a helpmeet to Portuguese students desiring to learn English. His guide makes it memorably clear he didn't know English; and—more important—that he probably bravely created his unwitting classic by utilizing, or going back and forth between, (1) a Portuguese-French phrase book and (2) a French-English dictionary. Linguistically, his reach so exceeded his grasp that he left posterity a comic masterpiece of misguided English.

Mark Twain loved Carolino's little book, and an introduction he wrote to it says there can be no question of the authenticity and sincerity of its "miraculous stupidities." "One cannot open this book anywhere," Twain says, "and not find richness." The richness includes misspellings and mispunctuations, but that's not the half of it. Pedro starts off with some "Familiar Phrases," including (for space reasons, I run them together there "horizontally"—they are even more enjoyable in the vertical, phrasebook format) these:

Go to send for. Have you say that? At what o'clock dine him? Apply you at the study during that you are young. Dress your hairs. Sing an area. This room is filled of bugs. This girl have a beauty edge. It is a noise which to cleave the head. Dry this wine. He has spit in my coat. I am catched cold in the brain. The thunderbolt is falling down. Dont you are awaken yet? Take that boy and whip him to much. Take care to dirt you self. The hands itch at him. Will some mutton? You not make who to babble.

Senhor Carolino also divides his book into "Familiar Dialogues." For example, "For make a visit in the morning":

Is your master at home?

Yes, sir.

Is it up?

No, sir, he sleep yet.

I go make that he get up.

It come in one's? How is it, you are in bed yet?

Yesterday at evening, I was to bed so late that I may not rising me soon that morning.

Well! what you have done after the supper?

We have sung, danced, laugh and played.

What game?

To the picket.

Whom I am sorry do not have know it!

Who have prevailed upon?

I had gained ten lewis.

Till at what o'clock its had play one?

As they say today, no one, except Pedro Carolino, could make this stuff up.

What is it that makes the difference between merely bad, sloppy, error-ridden English and wonderfully amusing xeno-English?

From Pedro Carolino to the present-day instructions that come with Japanese electronic products and "En-

glish" menus or hotel signs in very un-English-speaking
countries, fractured English mostly defies analysis: one
or two sentences of it may not, but beyond that one is
usually in a magical never-never land. The difference
between ordinary incorrect English and xeno-English is
possibly that while with mere incorrect English you can
usually single out a common error, with xeno-English it
is more often a case of wrong word order ("I want not a
pendulum"), a wrong synonym ("vessel captain" for
"ship's captain"), or remarkably bizarre sentence structure ("A day came a man consult this philosopher for to
know at o'clock it was owe to eat"). Another trait is the
frequent misuse of minor words, such as articles and
prepositions.

But Pedro Carolino's sentences cover the gamut of
possible slips—for example, lack of verb and subject
agreement ("Take care that he not give you a foot
kicks"); misuse of a word ("Wax my shoes"); wrong or
nonexistent inflection ("He was fighted"); unnecessary
words ("How do you can it to deny?"); misspellings or
nonexistent words ("the quater-grandmother"); and the
wrong part of speech ("If you like, I will hot it").

Between native incorrect English and fractured English is broken English: "Why you no help me?" Broken
English has omissions, choppy rhythms, a helpless de-
pendency on nouns, pronouns, verbs, and simple adjectives with other elements left out. Some of *New Guide of
the Conversation in Portuguese and English* could be
mere broken English, but most of the breakage is too
miraculous for that. Instead of "Why you no help me?"
he gives us "Why you no helps me to?"

Let us be thankful for the joys of xeno-English. It
creates its own skewed medium. It shows us how delightful language errors can be when they're original,
surprising, unpredictable. It is a special kind of English
because we feel the shadow of another tongue behind
its efforts. (If you want to treat yourself to some convul-
sively inane English—though the original is in French—
of the conversation-guide variety, if not so blessedly

mad as Pedro's English, see or read Eugene Ionesco's little play *The Bald Soprano*.)

Maybe you're a native speaker of English—and know at least one other language—and would like to try your hand at composing some authentic-sounding xeno-English. Remember that Pedro Carolino probably used only (1) a Portuguese-French phrase book and (2) a French-English dictionary to create his conversation guide. Try to forget that you know English (it's not that hard—millions of Americans succeed in doing it every day). In composing xeno-English, stick rigidly to your sources, those two bilingual dictionaries or phrase books. Don't be afraid to translate *very* literally.

The deliberately misspelled word in last week's column was *infinitessimal*. It's *infinitesimal*.

TERMS OF YOUR SENTENCE

WORD OF THE WEEK: *marrowsky*—a spoonerism, or initial-letter confusion

QUOTE OF THE WEEK: "Write something, even if it's just a suicide note."

—ANONYMOUS

Here is Exhibit One (it's the only one, actually) before you are briefly, and I hope informatively, sentenced here:

"The first time I laid eyes on Terry Lennox he was drunk in a Rolls-Royce Silver Wraith outside the terrace of The Dancers. The parking lot attendant had brought the car out and he was still holding the door open because Terry Lennox's left foot was still dangling outside, as if he had forgotten he had one. He had a young-looking face but his hair was bone white. You could tell by his eyes that he was plastered to the hairline, but otherwise he looked like any other nice young guy in a dinner jacket who had been spending too much money in a joint that exists for that purpose and no other."

These are the opening words of a novel, Raymond Chandler's *The Long Goodbye,* as handy as any to refer to for a little look this week at that unit of measure for speech that we call the sentence.

You are, when you write, nothing less than a composer. You are a composer of prose, but more fundamentally a composer of, one by one, sentences.

Sentences can be more interesting to study than you might think. Terminology, as always, helps when you want to understand the workings of something.

For example, what would you imagine that the terms *parataxis, anacoluthon,* and *synesis* forbiddingly refer to? To a lawyer's writ of habeus corpus? No, to parts of the body—the sentence body.

Learning these and just a few other terms will put you ahead of the mere Word Lover. It will make you a full-fledged Doctor of Sentences, a sharp-eyed diagnostician of those little or long units of complete thought we are always stringing together, whether obliviously, painfully, or joyfully.

A sentence is, the dictionary tells us (but let's simplify), a grammatical unit of words used in a relational (or syntactic) way and expressing an assertion *(declarative)*, a question *(interrogative)*, a command *(imperative)*, a wish *(optative)*, or an exclamation *(exclamatory)*. In writing, it begins with a capital letter and ends usually but by no means always with a period. We're talking basic grammar so far, but we live in days when not a lot of basic grammar is being earnestly talked or taught.

The *simple sentence* is composed of single clause. In the above Chandler passage, there is none, but "The parking lot attendant had brought the car out" (if the sentence ended there) would be a simple sentence, and so would "He had a young-looking face." An example of a *compound sentence,* or one with two main (independent or stand-aloneable) clauses, is "He had a young-looking face but his hair was bone white." The *complex sentence* has one main clause and at least one subordinate (dependent, or needing the rest of the sentence to make sense) clause, like the first one above: "The first time I laid eyes on Terry Lennox he was drunk in a Rolls-Royce Silver Wraith outside the terrace of The Dancers." The first clause is the dependent one. Then there's the *compound-complex sentence,* which has two main clauses and at least one subordinate one, like the final one above: "You could tell by his eyes that he was plastered to the hairline, but otherwise he looked like any other nice young guy in a dinner jacket who had been spending too much money in a joint that exists for that purpose and no other." Here, after two main clauses, the "who had been" clause is the subordinate one.

What you don't want to perpetrate is either a *run-on sentence* or a *squinting sentence* (or *squinting construction*). A run-on sentence is one, without a conjunction, that should stop or pause between clauses but doesn't, like "He had a young-looking face his hair was bone white." A squinting sentence is one with an ambiguous ingredient, ambiguous because the reader can't be sure which other part (before or after) it refers to. For example, "I decided Terry Lennox was drunk when I got there." Does this mean "I" made the decision about drunkenness when "I" got there, or that "I" realized Terry Lennox had reached the point of drunkenness when "I" got there? It's a squinter.

There are also incomplete sentences, but you might not know that grammatically there are two categories. The *sentence fragment* is self-explanatory. If, above, Raymond Chandler began, "The first time I" and stopped, you'd have a sentence fragment, an utterance or phrasing with no subject or predicate and lacking full meaning. But what if it makes sense? What if Chandler wrote, "Terry Lennox. Drunk in a Rolls-Royce Silver Wraith"? Both examples are elliptical, or missing something, but they make sense in their abbreviated way. They are *minor sentences,* or *elliptical sentences* (H. W. Fowler), like those we use every day: "Absolutely not." "In a way." "If you say so."

And then there are unfinished, rather than fragmentary sentences, and for diagnostic-sounding terms you can't do better than *aposiopesis* (pronunciation stress on the "pe") and *anacoluthon* (on the "lu"), two rhetoric terms you may remember from college if you majored in

English. An aposiopesis is a breaking off, as if the author above began, "The first time I laid eyes on Terry Lennox he—," then didn't finish the sentence, for one reason or another not wanting to proceed. When there's a midcourse shift—the initial grammatical setup doesn't follow through—it's a case of anacoluthon, as if the opening sentence above went, "The story about Terry Lennox—that first time, he was drunk in a Rolls-Royce Silver Wraith outside the terrace of The Dancers." These terms may be difficult, but we hear and commit aposiopeses and anacolutha every day.

You've also been speaking and writing both *loose sentences* and *periodic sentences*. These are deceptive terms that have nothing to do with speaking loosely or writing periodically (and that even most writers and editors today aren't familiar with—but should be). A loose sentence is one of those in which a thought (or statement) is completed before the sentence ends, with additional or subordinate clauses following that main clause. All the sentences in *The Long Goodbye* passage above are loose sentences, leading off with a subject and predicate. A periodic sentence, on the other hand, comes together—or becomes grammatically complete—only at its end. Rearrange the sentence "He had a young-looking face but his hair was bone white" to read "He had, although his hair was bone white, a young-looking face," and we've turned a loose sentence into a periodic one.

Another kind of sentence is the kind that is literally loose, that seems to proceed without any sense of order or forethought: "We went over there but they weren't home so we headed back to the restaurant since we thought they might be there." These are the snowballing sentences, with successive, tagged-on clauses or phrases that sometimes seem like afterthoughts but won't stop. English teachers don't like them at all. There's no formal term for them, but they've been called variously *decapitable sentences, accordion sentences, trailers,* and *stringy sentences* but not, correctly, *loose sentences*.

It's not surprising that the above Chandler excerpt has loose sentences. It's from a famous private-eye novel, and loose sentences go with the so-called *hard-boiled style,* whose characteristics are flat and dispassionate prose, unsentimental directness or brusque laconicism. The word *laconic* is from the place in ancient Greece called Laconia and means the very same thing as *Spartan. Atticism,* another English word we've borrowed from Greek, refers to elegant or witty conciseness in a phrase or sentence.

A sentence is words. It is also, except for the elementary or responsary kind, an opportunity, a pick of possibilities, a chance to arrange and emphasize those words in the best way. It is truly a little artistic composition, and it needn't always be composed by the rules. *Constructio ad sensum* ("construction according to sense") is what you call framing a sentence not strictly according to conventional syntax but intuitively and understandably. Another term for this is *synesis.* (The similar word *synchysis* refers to confused sentence arrangement. The great H. W. Fowler merely calls an ill-advised switch in sentence construction "swapping horses.") Similarly, a word can be considered in its own right or according to proper inflection or conjugation, a *paradigmatic* viewpoint; or contextually or syntactically, in terms of the words it is joined with, a *syntagmatic.* Never forget syntagmatics. A word's meaning comes not so much from the dictionary as from how it is used, how often it is used, and the verbal company it keeps.

Talk about sentences, and you're soon talking about prose style. The two key words here are *hypotaxis* (adjective *hypotactic)* and *parataxis* (adjective *paratactic).* Sentence style using connectives (conjunctions) and dependent clauses is called hypotaxis. If you write in a full and varied or even sophisticated style, you are a hypotactic writer. But then there is that spare, one-simple-sentence-after-another prose style, coordinate rather than conjunctive. No *and*s, *if*s, or *but*s about it, it's a paratactic style. If the Chandler passage were to be rewritten in a strict paratactic mode, it would read: "I remember the first time I laid eyes on Terry Lennox. He was drunk in a Rolls-Royce Silver Wraith outside the terrace of The Dancers. The parking lot attendant had brought the car out. He was still holding the door open. Terry Lennox's left foot was still dangling outside. It was as if he had forgotten he had one. He had a young-looking face. But his hair was bone white." And so forth.

Your writing style can be complicated or it can be simple. A sophisticated style, using rhetorical devices and elaborate sentences, with suspensions or inversions, is sometimes called a *mandarin style*. A plain style is called—the *plain style*. An old-fashioned style, as for a historical novel, is a *period style*.

If you're a language-watcher, try to take note not only of words per se but also of sentences. You'll learn the joy of crafting an individual sentence, then of following that with another sentence that gets a "flow" going. When you appreciate the satisfactions of a simple, consistent string of sentences as well as those of a more complex ordering of varied types of sentences, you begin to appreciate the art of prose style.

It all starts with thinking of yourself as a verbal composer. Be kind to your sentences. Maybe we should all think less about parallel universes and more about parallel structure.

The deliberately misspelled word in last week's column was *turniquet*. It's *tourniquet*.

USAGE ROUNDUP

WORD OF THE WEEK: *tertium quid*—a "third" something other than two opposites

QUOTE OF THE WEEK: "One forgets words as one forgets names. One's vocabulary needs constant fertilization or it will die."

—EVELYN WAUGH

Aren't people wrong who use *infer* to mean *imply?* Can it ever be correct to use *between,* rather than *among,* when more than two things are involved? Is it acceptable that *disinterested* is now frequently being used to mean *uninterested?*

It's usage roundup time, and it's quite a large herd.

Is there a right and wrong in all questions of language?

The latter question was a starting point in the year's first and earliest Wordwizard column. I tried to shine a little flashlight on some of the issues and complications underlying linguistic right and wrong (if there is such a thing), but that human hunger for simple and definite answers never seems to go away.

It may always come down to this: Different answers for different fanciers.

But the column today will close with a little capsule review of issues that language purists typically feel strongly about—and a hint that they should probably feel less strongly, or at least less dogmatically, about them.

The above questions regarding *infer* and *imply, between* and *among,* and *disinterested* and *uninterested* are among many I've received (and attempted to answer, if not within this column) from Woofton readers. These in particular are perennials, along with twenty or thirty others. Year after year, they're asked again and again by countless people, addressed again and again in numerous books, and reargued again and again by language columnists and their readers. That these hotly debated issues over certain words and usages always seem to remain unsettled tells us something.

It tells us that there usually is no simple answer for each—at least, not one that will satisfy everybody.

To be an authority in such disputes, you must first have an authority, and there's the rub. Should that authority be a particular book or dictionary, and if so which one? Should it be the Latin language, on which so many "correct" English usages are based? Should it be England, where our language comes from? Or should it be grammarians of late-nineteenth and early-twentieth-century America, from whom many of our latter-day usage "rules" come?

Should it be the past, a sense of tradition, a respect for literary precedents? Or should it be the present, tradition be damned: However people are speaking and writing today, that's what's correct?

Another complication in the way of absolute answers is the fact that a word often has more than one meaning (so-called polysemy); similarly, the meanings of two controversially confused words can overlap. Another is that it turns out that some similar words now considered different in meaning, such as *mantle* and *mantel,* were originally merely spelling variants.

Our ever-changing language, that is, is like a floodplain of words, with their meanings often freezing, thawing, freezing again, thawing again. Or you could say that words gravitate to the wrong people and fall right into their lapse.

If you think history or historical precedent is the important thing here, another interesting problem arises: How far back in history do you find your authority, particularly if there has been a "back and forth" about the issue over the centuries?

Think of your friends, acquaintances, and teachers. Would they all support only one of the above points of view? Not likely.

If you read—or even see—enough books on English usage, you'll be well advised to realize that the salient consideration word isn't *right* or *correct.* It's *distinction.*

In most cases where the meanings of two "often confused" expressions is in dispute, what it comes down to is whether you're a person who likes to preserve fine distinctions between word meanings or one who thinks such differentiations are pedantic and not worth worrying about. The same in the case of a single controversial word, which may have an older, stricter meaning as well as a newer, looser meaning. Distinction or nondistinction, that is the question. Do you favor, for example, always using *farther* in spatial contexts and *further* in abstract or figurative senses? *Admittance* for physical entrance and *admission* for other, less premise-specific entrees?

If you're a militant distinction-preserver, you're a purist, a language conservative, a prescriptivist, possibly an authoritarian. You want to fix the language, in both senses of that word. If you can't stand such cherished fine points about simple speech, see them as undemocratic, and think that the fact that so many other people don't bother about such peccadilos is good enough for you, you're a language liberal, either a descriptivist (meaning that proper usage is what is and can be described, not what's prescribed) or—a somewhat pejorative term—a permissivist.

If you're a person "of distinction," you know that such matters also separate the guardians from the abusers. You are aware of particular "wrong" usages and tend to be a little judgmental toward those oblivious to the distinctions you want to safeguard. On the other hand, most language scholars and easygoing utterers consider these jealously guarded distinctions shibboleths, or nothing more than tired debatable criteria for those who like to be a little snobbish.

Still, one can be in favor of distinguishing between *disinterested* and *uninterested* without being hoity-toity or "elitist." Some distinctions are worth practicing, so to speak, especially when clarity will otherwise be blurred or when alternatives (synonyms) are wanting. More pragmatically, many caring speakers and writers find it well advised to abide by the shibboleths of right and wrong, if only to avoid being regarded as somebody unconscious or sloppy about language matters. That is, in speech too, appearance can definitely be important.

Whatever your emotions about language issues (and they can be emotional issues), what you don't want to be is both opinionated and totally ignorant regarding the histories or complexities of the words in question. Too many people—including language "experts"—today manage very comfortably to be both.

One way you can keep yourself from being foolishly rigid is by buying a copy of *Webster's Dictionary of English Usage*. This comprehensive and commonsensical reference outdoes all previous usage guides because, first, it reviews the historical evidence and arguments in each case; and, second, it is not, like almost all other usage guides, a rhapsody of dos and don'ts that boil down to the author's own self-justified preferences and pet peeves.

In short, everybody's entitled to personal predilections, but a little responsibility should go along with it: the responsibility to use a dictionary and read up a little on how word meanings evolve over time.

Here, as a reward for your pledge to do a little boning up in *Webster's Dictionary of English Usage* before becoming opinionated, is a touch-upon roundup—if not a final resolution—of many of the classic, canonical issues of contemporary English usage. "Classic" meaning they show up in just about every modern usage guide from Fowler's *Modern English Usage* on and sometimes are touched on in general dictionaries.

If you are a zealous, jealous grammar-and-usage traditionalist who deplores the misuse of certain words, some of the following are probably your favorite causes for making careful, respectful distinctions between words.

The good news is you have some legitimate gripes and lots of company.

The bad news—are you sitting down?—is that, in virtually all these cases, a look back at the history of the words in question will give you surprising and disappointing revelations.

Look into the *Oxford English Dictionary* or *Webster's Dictionary of English Usage,* and you'll find that the "misuse" you decry dates back quite a few decades, if not centuries; or that the violent objections to it are of relatively recent date and derive from misguided schoolmarm notions; or that more famous, respected writers have used that misuse more often than you can bear to know about.

Item:

That *admittance,* not *admission,* should always be used in the sense of physical entrance: Many great writers have never observed this distinction.

That *awhile,* written as one word, should never be used after the preposition *for* (or before *ago* or *back),* when it should be *a while:* The distinction isn't always easily made, as when the *for* is omitted or understood, and the *Oxford English Dictionary* has examples of *for awhile* from the nineteenth century.

That *between* should never be used as a preposition, instead of *among,* when more than two things are involved: It's been so used for centuries.

That *anxious* ("feeling worry") should never be used

to mean *eager* ("desirous"): Writers have used the words interchangeably since the early 1800s.

That *between you and I* (rather than *me*) is grammatically wrong: It was used many centuries ago, and by England's Restoration dramatists and Mark Twain.

That *careen* (for a wavering motion, originally a nautical term) should not be carelessly used for *career* (for headlong motion): Many recent American writers have "broadened" its meaning to the point of its being a synonym.

That *cohort* ("a group or band") should not be misused to mean what *comrade* or *associate* means: The borrowed meaning is indeed a recent American doing, but how many speakers or writers today use *cohort* in its original collective sense?

That the whole *comprises* the parts, not the parts the whole: Whether the word is used actively or passively *(is comprised of)* is a factor here.

That *continual* ("repeated or intermittent") should not be confused with *continuous* ("steady and unbroken"): The distinction seems not to have existed before the mid-nineteenth century.

That *convince* should be followed only by *of,* never (like *persuade)* by *to,* or an infinitive: The use with *to* is indeed recent. You may be convinced of your stand on this, but how many of the other 99 percent of the populace can you convince not to use *to?*

That *decimate* ("to kill one-tenth of a group") should not be used for the broader meanings of "seriously devastate" or "deplete": Going back to the seventeenth century, the word has rarely been used with its original Roman army meaning.

That it's always *different from,* not *different than:* Actually, *different to* or *unto* was the earliest usage: *Different than* was first used in 1644 and later, in the eighteenth century, by Oliver Goldsmith.

That *due to* (rather than *owing to* or *because of*) should never be used adverbially, only prepositionally:

There was no grammatical objection to this until early in this century.

That *enormity* ("something gravely outrageous or monstrous") does not mean the same thing as *enormousness* ("hugeness"): It's been pointed out that those two meanings can overlap and that there is no historical basis for the distinction.

That *farther,* not *further,* should be used when it is a question of physical distance: They've long been used interchangeably.

That in talking of poor health or of regret, it's properly *feel bad,* not *feel badly:* Both expressions are widely used, possibly because an 1869 handbook recommended *feel badly* and later schoolbooks favored *feel bad.* (Curiously, we always think badly, not bad, of someone.)

That *flaunt* ("to display ostentatiously") is not interchangeable with *flout* ("to disregard deliberately"): This indeed is an error, but many writers and intellectuals today are perpetuating it.

That *fortuitous* (occurring by chance) should not be used to mean what *fortunate* conveys: The words' meanings have not always been clear-cut—there can be overlap—and some uses of *fortuitous* in the eighteenth century had overtones of implied good fortune.

That *infer* ("to deduce") ought not be used after a personal subject to mean what *imply* means: The usage history of these two words is *very* complicated, and a rashly oversimplified opinion is unwise.

That *masterful* ("domineering") is not interchangeable with *masterly* ("skillful or expert"): There was no such clear distinction in usage of the two words until the great H. W. Fowler propounded one in 1926.

That as an introductory phrase, it's *more important,* not *more importantly:* Grammatical defenses for both are possible, and *Webster's Dictionary of English Usage* notes that even contemporary usage authorities have been known to use both forms.

That *nauseous* ("causing nausea") should not be confused with *nauseated* ("feeling nausea"): In fact, *nau-*

seous has been used in three different senses since the seventeenth century.

That *none* ("no one") must be followed only by a singular verb, never by a plural one: It has been used with both kinds of verbs since the fourteenth century.

That *over* should never be used to mean the same thing as *more than:* It has been used in this quantitative sense since the fourteenth century.

That *partially* ("with favoritism or a bias") should never be used in place of *partly* ("to some degree or not completely"): They've been used interchangeably since the fifteenth century.

That *proven* is not the valid past participle of *prove*— only *prove* is: *Proven* does indeed derive from Scottish *preven,* but countless modern writers have so used *proven*—or both forms at different times.

That *transpire* ("to become known or leak out") ought never be used as a synonym for *happen* or *occur:* It was so used as early as 1814.

All of which goes to show that being right isn't as easy as it's cracked up to be.

If history is the final authority, a look back at the verbal record usually shows that "answers" in usage are anything but hard and fast. From a little language research, you'll even learn that *it's,* our verbal contraction with an apostrophe, was used for the possessive *its* in the seventeenth and eighteenth centuries.

Let all these less-than-absolute findings be a lesson to us: to keep in mind always that a living, irregular, ever-evolving language, English, will never have the comforting consistent, defining order of a stylebook.

But don't let this stop you from being a finicky foot soldier for fine points of language, a person of distinctions.

If you are such a person, don't forget: You're also supposed to oppose strongly that awful word *hopefully,* deplore the brainless new intrusions of *like,* favor *kudos* as a singular rather than a plural and *media* as a plural rather than a singular, uphold the pejorative meaning of *fulsome,* allow the use of *dilemma* only when there are two options, and preserve the important distinctions between *torturous* and *tortuous, trouper* and *trooper, turbid* and *turgid.* . . . It's all enough to make one discomfited. Or is it discomforted?

The deliberately misspelled word in last week's column was *habeus corpus.* It's *habeas corpus.*

MYSTERY CLIPS

WORD OF THE WEEK: *scientism*—a questionable science approach to a nonscience

QUOTE OF THE WEEK: "The knowledge of words is the gate of scholarship."

—JOHN WILSON

How would you feel about subjecting yourself to some fore-clipping? Why not? Words do it every day.

Talk about fore-clipping may seem to be apellous (circumcision-related) or tonsorial (haircut-related), but it's not. It's language talk, specifically having to do with the shortening of words by lopping off a syllable or two from either the back end or the front end.

It's the loss of back ends that's the main subject here.

Take the sentence "I told her on the phone that I liked the news photo of the co-op, but that the ad gave no detailed info about the drapes or how comfy the place was, the trustworthy super, the auto garage, the building's gym facilities, or the nearby bus stop." Few of us would notice that twelve of this sentence's forty-seven words are shortenings of other English words. We use these shorter words so often, they're so familiar to us, that—the fact catches us short.

Such words as *phone, news, photo, co-op, ad, info, drapes, comfy, super, auto, gym,* and *bus* are called clipped forms. They're also variously called shortened forms, clipped words, curtailed words, and stump words. Whatever these syllable-ectomized words are known as, word-shortening is a characteristic, colorful, informalizing aspect of English. As with slang in conversation, we scarcely give it a thought.

The technical term for clipping the back ends of vocables—*examination* into *exam, ammunition* into *ammo, champion* into *champ*—is apocope. Clipping the front ends off—getting *pike* from *turnpike, pop* from *soda pop, Vegas* from *Las Vegas, Nam* from *Vietnam* or *Viet Nam, copter* from *helicopter, kraut* from *sauerkraut, gator* from *alligator, bus* from *omnibus, van* from *caravan, still* from *distillery, sport* from *disport, wig* from *periwig*—is apheresis.

But the term *clipped form* is nicely understandable for those many words that could be described as the fast food of English. They're bite-sized but still give the full taste of meaning. Either the vanished syllable (or syllables) is understood, for example, *rhino(ceros);* or it's dropped away so long ago that we may not even know the word's original full form—for example, *grog,* which comes indirectly from *grogam,* meaning "cloak," which was part of the nickname, Old Grog, for a particular British admiral of the eighteenth century.

Abbreviation, of course, is the broader category of this phenomenon. There are different theories and time estimates as to when humankind's first word was uttered. Whenever the first word came forth, the first abbreviation can't have been far behind. Compressing or economizing utterance—or is it impatience or laziness? —seems to be a natural instinct.

Abbreviation is especially useful, and space-saving, in written English. To save paper and not be-letter the obvious, we depend greatly on bureaucratic initialisms, such as *IRS, CIA,* and *FDA;* and acronyms (or pronounceable initialisms), such as *NATO, NAFTA,* and *radar.* Initialese also comes in handy for mnemonics, or shortcuts for remembering particular facts. Scuba divers, for example, memorize "Roy G. Biv" for the order in which perceived colors disappear as one dives deeper.

We also recombine or squash words into blend words (also known as portmanteau words, centaur words, and telescope words), such as *brunch* from *breakfast* and *lunch.* Contractions are a standard way of eliminating letters, whether in common forms of address or honorifics *(Mrs., Rev., Dr.)* or in the verb forms *(don't, can't, wouldn't)* we learn about in school, which eliminate letters but generate a few apostrophes.

The initialized abbreviations are especially rife in the domains of government, the military, science (and measurement), law enforcement, and non-face-to-face communications in general. They're the shorthand of on-the-job urgency, or sometimes, more self-consciously, just on-the-job jargon. But we also pare our words down to initials in everyday life—think only of how familiar *CD, ID, ASAP, FYI, TLC, BYO, S&M, DJ,* and *PO'd* are. Speaking of *PO'd,* what do you call a "softened" off-color initialism, such as *SOB* or *BS?* You call it a eusystolism, or at least H. L. Mencken did (but try to find it in a dictionary).

Clipped forms, though, seem a little more organic a part of our language than do the artificial, spare, code-like discontinuities of alphabet soup, particularly because so many clippings have such common use, from stevadores to executives, in our spoken language and informal written language. Generally speaking, rather than being canny abbreviating concoctions, they develop more naturally as words in their own right. A syllable or two gets dropped along the wayside over time, and sometimes becomes completely forgotten. Their genesis is usually impatient, irreverent—and often very American. Not surprisingly, many of them begin as fresh, zippy coinages but become part of mainstream English, losing their "slang" or "informal" or "colloquial" dictionary label. It makes for quickened English in both senses of that adjective: quicker and livelier.

Among back-clipped words we hear everywhere today

(and that need no explanation or "filling out" here to be understood) are *grad, beaut, medic, coon, sarge, dorm, gent, prof, hi-fi, biz, porn, noncom, obit, cuke, nuke, civvies, sax, combo, prez, tarp, dipso, legit, hippo, mayo, lit, teen, prefab, sec, prep, syph, psycho, pard, vibes, tux, bra, fax, celeb, bod, dupe,* (copy), *commish, divvy, sit-com, prelim, temp, spec, specs, hankie, deli, memo, alum, jeans, natch,* and *letch.* You'll notice that in some cases there's a letter change at the end that shores up the clipped form, as with *prez, hankie, fax, natch,* and *letch.*

There are also some doubles among clipped forms: *vet(eran)* and *vet(erinarian), rep(resentative)* and *rep(utation),* and *quad(rangle)* and *quad(riplegic).* (There also used to be *quad* for *quadriphonic.*) How about a triple: *con(vict), con(fidence trick),* and *con(tra).* And needful to mention, sometimes whole words get clipped: *Do you have cable (television)?*

Already you're through this sample list and thinking of more. Think no more. There are some more coming here, and they're the interesting ones: clipped forms with a mysterious past.

Mysterious past? I refer to a number of common shortened words that everybody uses but whose original, longer versions are less obvious. Knowing them—or guessing them—should not be so difficult as knowing the etymological origins (from other languages) of words. Here the front end of the derivation is sticking out, so to speak. This little advantage makes it all the more interesting, I venture to say, that many of us *still* won't be able to guess the original words from which these stumps come.

If we're abbreviating, doesn't it behoove us to know at least what we've abbreviated?

Here is a sampling of mysterious clipped forms. For how many of them can you supply the longer word that was shortened? (Answers in following paragraph.)

Clipped forms: *brig, mob, props, spats, cab, cinema, curio, pants, dynamo, cent, pub, zoo, sap* ("fool"), *semi* (truck), *bunk, pep, gat, bum, gin, ad lib, piano, miss, hobby, fan, blitz, hype, razz, rube, vamp, wiener, sync, perk, gab, flip,* and *boob.*

Extra credit (tough ones): *patter, squash, rum, wag,* and *whisky.*

(Answers: *brigantine, mobile vulgus, properties, spatterdashes, cabriolet, cinematograph, curiosity, pantaloons, dynamo-electric machine, centum, public house, zoological gardens, saphead, semitrailer, buncombe, pepper* or *pepsin, Gatling gun, bummer, geneva, ad libetum, pianoforte, mistress, hobby horse, fanatic, blitzkrieg, hyperbole* or *hypodermic, raspberry, Reuben, vampire, wienerwurst, synchronization/synchronism, perquisite, gabble, flippant,* and *booby.*)

Extra credit (tough ones): *paternoster, askutasquash, rumbullion, waghalter,* and *usquebaugh.*

The deliberately misspelled word in last week's column was *pecadillos.* It's *peccadillos.*

MOVIE PUFFCORN

WORD OF THE WEEK: *esprit de l'escalier*—wishful wit that one didn't show

QUOTE OF THE WEEK: "The feeling for words comes at an early age—or rather it is lost in most cases at an early age, leaving the rest poets."

—PETER DE VRIES

Would you be interested in an invaluable pocket verbal chart that will give you all the words you need to become a movie critic?

But first, it's movie night. Which movie will you see? You're scanning those movie posters with their blurbs outside the Cine-Qua-Nine-Plex theater and trying to decide which movie is for you.

Will it be the drama *Terms of Rapprochement* ("Powerful." "A major event and explosive must-see blockbuster.")?

Then there's the new epical fantasy with great special effects, *The Diamond Thimble* ("Magical!" "A feast for the senses!").

But playing just on the other side of the thin wall from *The Diamond Thimble* is the latest thriller, *Lethal Rejection* ("A heart-stopping dynamite wow of a nail-biter roller-coaster!" "A sizzling home run!").

At Theater 4, however, there's the comedy *Dweebie's World II* ("A goof of a spoof!" "Laugh-out-loud funny!").

But four escalator rides down, at Theater 5, is another comedy, *Crude Habits* ("Two thumbs erect!" "Fall-over-dead funny!").

A comedy sounds just right, but which one? One of them is laugh-out-loud funny. The other one is fall-over-dead funny. Both blurbs are quotes from the same movie critic. Wouldn't fall-over-dead funny be funnier? Or . . .

This little dilemma (or multiplex-lemma) is hypothetical, but the language of movie advertising in America is not hypothetical. It's hyperbolic, and it's always coming right at us. True enough, many people choose a movie casually because of its title, its star, a noisy and juiced-up trailer (or preview), the quiet recommendation of a friend, or the waggling thumbs-up of critics Tweedledee and Tweedledum on television.

But there are also those big print ads in the newspaper.

They may have suggestive pictures or "theme" symbols and provocative catchphrases (say, "An erotic no-man's-land—until she taught him the facts of death!"). Theme image or not, they almost always have blurbs.

Blurbs, or puffs, are brief endorsements. In the case of American movie advertising, they're spasms of critical, or less than critical, appreciation usually worked into a ringing phrase, sometimes rounded off with an exclamation point. Come-in lines, if you will, rather than come-on lines. When a film is being released, the order goes out to those publicists: Round up all the usual adjectives; better yet, some unusual ones—but not too unusual.

The puffs are usually massed to create a page-filling assault of raving excerpts from movie reviewers and critics. (Reviewers like to puff, while critics prefer to puncture.) Alliteration is often afoot: "Fiercely funny!" "Warm and winsome!" "Tinglingly tense and taut!" Or a bit of rhyme without good reason: "A groovy movie!" "A soundly made and played film." "Immeasurably pleasurable!" If they don't make the point, there are always those points of ecphonesis, otherwise known as exclamation points.

Puffs are never negative, of course. We read of towering achievements, never cringing or huddling ones. A movie is always a home run, never a scratch single. It's a must-see, never a must-see-through. It never lets up rather than never gets started, and you'll always leave the theater beaming, not boiling. Certainly it's never one-thumb-up. (You should know, by the way, that the gladiatorial-combat-derived term *thumbs up* is a "positive" misnomer: Historically, it was the Roman crowd's or emperor's thumbs down, for sword down, that saved the loser's life.)

But pity those all-thumbs movie reviewers. Adulatory adjectives were made to be overused. Even in the great and various English language, there are only so many descriptives and depictives to draw from. How to praise in a fresh way is a problem in all realms of art, or how to make art criticism artistic. Of stories and plots, it's proverbial that there is nothing new under the sun. It could also be said of film-blurbing (or -damning, for that matter) that there's nothing new to be noted under the projector's ray.

Look, for example, at movie ads extolling the performances and charisma of the actors and actresses. How many descriptives are there to draw upon? He or she is typically *compelling, vibrant, magnetic, irresistible, always believable, dashing, sexy, unforgettable, scintillating, amazing, appealing, superb, brilliant, ravishing, stunning, riveting* . . . He or she is *at the top of his/her form, gives the performance of the year,* or *lights up the screen.* The film *makes a star of* . . .

Besides individual adjectives, the language of movie advertising also depends on tried and true, single-sentence clichés. Look no further. Here are some of the classics, along with the exclamation points that usually follow them:

An unforgettable experience! The hit of the year! The film of the decade/season! Explodes across the big screen!

A milestone! A stunning achievement! A masterpiece! America's favorite ———! Makes ——— look like ———! Destined to have a permanent place in ———! Outdoes ———! Wow! A blockbuster! A winner! Don't miss it! A must-see! An experience! A powerhouse! It must be experienced! If you loved ———, you'll love ———! Best film of the year! One of the year's ten best! Packs a wallop! ——— at his best! Puts ——— on the map! ——— is in top form! A classic for the ages! One of the few ——— in recent years/memory to ———! Scores a knock-out! The most talked-about ———! Gets an A! Not for the faint of heart! You'll leave the theater ———! ———'s back! ——— delivers! Has hit written all over it! Great fun! Doesn't let up! An unmitigated joy! Have you seen it only once? Loads of fun! Experience it for yourself! An event! Will appeal to ——— and ——— alike! ——— scores! One of this year's ———! Check it out! Manages to be ——— without being ———! Sheer genius! Never to be forgotten! Pure pleasure! A sheer delight! Sheer magic! Sheer lunacy! Two thumbs up!

Do these look a little familiar?

Not that there haven't been some changes, or drop-outs, in the movie reviewer's bag of adjectives. Until the late 1960s or so, only certain films stood out as being notorious, usually for irreligious or sexual content deemed to be morally objectionable in the United States of America—and they were advertised that way to titillate and attract the curious public. A film was *shocking, controversial, revealing* (in the prurient sense), *scandalous, explicit, uncensored,* or *banned by the Catholic Church. Shame* was another big word, used shamelessly in ads. Even the terms *art film* or *a film from Europe* were ripe with suggestiveness to relatively puritanical America. (On the other hand, an *adult film*—or one on an *adult subject* or *adult theme*—back then usually meant an unusually *mature* one, dealing with a then-*bold* or self-consciously *controversial* subject, such as illegitimate children or racial prejudice.)

These stock puff adjectives of thirty and more years

ago tell us in a word(s) how innocent the movies and the
world were back then. Since then, taboos have gone
skidoo. But exhausting and exhausted cinema superlatives? They're still coming soon to your local motion
picture theater.

If we can't fight them, we might as well learn them
and thereby qualify immediately as movie reviewers
ourselves. I believe that studies here and there have
shown that while 70 percent of the youth in America
would like to become either film directors or actors and
make an Oscar acceptance speech at the Dorothy Chandler Pavillion, the remaining 30 percent would like to
become film critics or reviewers. If you're not one of
those 30 percent, you may still have some fun with the
handy six-column Movie Rave Key at the end of this
chapter.

To be a compleat, puffcorn-glib movie reviewer, you
must have an arsenal of adjectives. You must know how
to combine them for each kind of film, be it a drama,
spectacle, action or suspense film, or comedy. For example, ideally, a particular film should not be described
simply as "stirring." It should be lauded as "A wonderfully stirring experience." Or "A wonderfully stirring
and high-wire experience."

The following Movie Rave Key contains 450 words
arranged in six columns.

To create a movie rave line, use the simple left-to-
right formula: one adverb plus one adjective plus one
noun. Or two adjectives. Or three. Do you want a rave
for a Drama or Melodrama; Spectacle or Fantasy; Action or Suspense (thriller); or Comedy or Oddball film?
Choose your adverb, than the adjective(s) from the appropriate (or even inappropriate) column(s), then your
final noun.

The categorization of all these adjectives is by no
means rigid, nor could it be, and there's considerable
overlap. An adjective under the Spectacle or Fantasy
heading may be quite apt for a sci-fi action film, for
example. Similarly, an adverb in the left-hand column

can easily be borrowed for use as an adjective (not appearing in the other five columns), or vice versa.

Note that nouns for specific types of movie—sequel, prequel, debut, farce, tragicomedy, and the like—are not included in the (more general) key.

The need for compactness limits the film categories here to four. But many of these adjectives should serve for any other type of film (such as a western, musical, whodunit, or documentary). The possibilities are many and intriguing, and sometimes maybe even quite amusing.

The deliberately misspelled word in last week's column was *stevadores*. It's *stevedores*.

MOVIE RAVE KEY

	DRAMA OR MELODRAMA	SPECTACLE OR FANTASY	ACTION OR SUSPENSE	COMEDY OR ODDBALL	
1. remarkably	moving	beautiful	thrilling	amusing	film
2. utterly	powerful	magnificent	chilling	funny	movie
3. stunningly	touching	visionary	taut	comic	story
4. truly	sobering	magical	dynamite	hilarious	adventure
5. quite	unsparing	dreamlike	tense	droll	experience
6. hugely	stirring	sumptuous	high-energy	different	milestone
7. thoroughly	tender	sensuous	heart-pounding	outrageous	hit
8. vastly	forceful	colorful	heart-stopping	delirious	runaway hit
9. tremendously	impassioned	surreal	white-knuckle	uproarious	classic
10. wonderfully	emotional	dazzling	tension-packed	madcap	achievement
11. unprecedentedly	searing	lush	spine-tingling	nutty	gem
12. delightfully	provocative	eye-filling	adrenaline-pumping	loony	journey
13. wildly	incisive	spellbinding		zany	tale
14. extremely	penetrating	ravishing	slam-bang	rib-tickling	powerhouse
15. totally	charged	awesome	throbbing	side-splitting	triumph
16. flawlessly	wrenching	breathtaking	suspenseful	riotous	work of art
17. superbly	engrossing	sweeping	scary	wacked-out	feast for the senses

18. completely	worthwhile	lovely	high-wire	hysterical	masterpieces
19. immensely	riveting	mesmerizing	fast	loopy	grabber
20. unforgettably	intelligent	enchanting	violent	crazy	miracle of film
21. lovingly	first-rate	marvelous	fast-paced	insane	event
22. exceptionally	outstanding	gorgeous	tough	demented	smash
23. curiously	solid	amazing	steamroller of a	kooky	production
24. superbly	admirable	enjoyable	rollercoaster of a	bouncy	fable
25. brilliantly	groundbreaking	pleasurable	nail-biter of a	zesty	saga
26. uniquely	inspiring	rhapsodic	shoot-'em-up	quirky	time bomb
27. superlatively	gripping	stunning	erotic	bizarre	creation
28. appealingly	electrifying	idyllic	smoldering	unexpected	trip
29. engagingly	compelling	splendid	steamy	surprising	adventure
30. phenomenally	heartfelt	picturesque	sizzling	saucy	statement
31. perfectly	warm	entertaining	lusty	charming	blockbuster
32. toweringly	warmhearted	kaleidoscopic	sexy	offbeat	merry-go-round
33. terrifically	affirmative	enthralling	hot	sly	must-see
34. grandly	wise	astonishing	hot, hot, hot	refreshing	megahit
35. radiantly	sweet	evocative	white-hot	original	Oscar-contender
36. majestically	true-to-life	out-of-this-world	intense	weird	joy
37. quietly	feel-good	high-adventure	cool	rare	work of genius
38. expertly	romantic	awesome	seductive	fresh	home run
39. howlingly	passionate	imaginative	nonstop	unconventional	thriller

	DRAMA OR MELODRAMA	SPECTACLE OR FANTASY	ACTION OR SUSPENSE	COMEDY OR ODDBALL	
40. roaringly	raw	astounding	jolting	hard-edged	sleeper
41. absorbingly	earthy	monumental	kinetic	engaging	puzzler
42. delicately	uncompromising	extraordinary	stylish	hip	reenactment
43. radiantly	bold	exquisite	smart	sharp	smorgasbord
44. fiercely	devastating	mind-blowing	flashy	witty	fairy tale
45. tightly	haunting	eye-opening	no-holds-barred	savvy	wow
46. briskly	intriguing	storybook	zesty	black	slice of life
47. unusually	dark	epical	clever	brash	chronicle
48. for once	unflinching	imposing	slick	lively	yarn
49. daringly	gritty	rare	sensational	inventive	portrayal
50. enormously	momentous	fascinating	sleek	goofy	work
51. artistically	realistic	stately	classy	bright	winner
52. vividly	honest	atmospheric	original	screwball	romp
53. highly	priceless	grandiose	ingenious	laugh-out-loud	spoof
54. starkly	impressive	for-the-whole-family	diabolical	yummy	frolic
55. cinematically	shattering	great	relentless	breezy	knockout
56. screamingly	savage	luminous	pulsating	rambunctious	takeoff
57. simply	graphic	beguiling	arty	fall-over-dead funny	exploration

58. notably	special	wondrous	sophisticated	wicked	dramatization
59. sublimely	absorbing	phantasmagoric	flashy	happy	accomplishment
60. meticulously	unsentimental	historic	bone-chilling	merry	sensation
61. worthily	believable	big-scale	macabre	maniacal	shocker
62. crisply	illuminating	mind-bending	byzantine	off-the-wall	tour-de-force
63. inexpressibly	heartbreaking	extravagant	action-packed	fun-filled	pageant
64. elegantly	heartrending	landmark	rip-roaring	unlikely	concoction
65. smoothly	dramatic	seductive	mysterious	wacky	extravaganza
66. consummately	simple	lavish	scorching	irreverent	success
67. gloriously	searching	scenic	exciting	slapstick	bull's-eye
68. unabashedly	fine	enveloping	rousing	silly	portrait
69. broadly	captivating	hypnotic	explosive	drop-dead funny	lollapalooza
70. quaintly	sensitive	escapist	churning	spicy	award-winner
71. simply	well-done	elaborate	frightening	mischievous	odyssey
72. authentically	thought-provoking	lyrical	jarring	disarming	lark
73. startlingly	involving	good old-fashioned	fiendish	pleasant	hit
74. skillfully	affecting	eye-filling	potent	tongue-in-cheek	job
75. profoundly	insightful	large-canvas	punchy	upbeat	import

PINCHED POLITESSE AND
BOREDOM BUFFERS

WORD OF THE WEEK: *logomachy*—contention over words

QUOTE OF THE WEEK: "Great literature is simply language charged with meaning to the utmost possible degree."

—EZRA POUND

The American actor Charles Grodin tells of the time in England, while awaiting a camera setup for a movie being shot at a castle, that he and an actress momentarily sat down in one of the castle's side rooms. An Englishwoman appeared and asked if they had been asked to wait in that room. When they replied no, she said, "Well, it would be so nice if you weren't here."

Our language—and day-to-day dealings with one another—is full of it-would-be-so-nice-if-you-weren't-here expressions.

"I beg your *pardon?*" one person says with a questioning inflection when crowded against the back of an elevator. "I beg *your* pardon," the other person says, whom somebody else crowded.

Now, they both say "I beg your pardon." But the tones and emphases make it clear that neither is begging any pardon at all. The first person is really saying, "What do you think you're doing, pushing me against the wall?" The other is saying, "You're crowding me,

too, and this pushing isn't my fault, so don't blame me."
Hostile? Well, at least, not enthusiastic.

Clearly, comments aren't always meant literally. This
is especially obvious in the case of sarcasm or sardonicism, a kind of pointed overstatement. The person who
says, "What a lovely sight you are" to somebody covered
with mud or foolish clothing doesn't mean that at all.
Similarly, there's irony, where there's another level of
meaning beyond the verbal apparent one; and there are
understatement and double meaning.

But more subtle than the word-versus-meaning play
of sarcasm, irony, understatement, and double meaning
are those seemingly polite or harmless expressions we
use all the time but don't—always or usually or sometimes—exactly mean, from *I beg your pardon* to *Of
course you're not imposing.* With these reflexive comments, the issue is not so much utter falseness or
pointed animosity. Even a simple *No thank you* is often
said pointedly, with no thankfulness at all. It's *what's
really going on* socially and psychologically. They're our
hollow polite-isms, our unmeant amenities.

And not a one of us could live without them.

We have so many ritual expressions that on the surface are quite ordinary, pleasant, and courteous but are
really handy masks over less-than-friendly feelings. If
they're not black-hearted, they're at least half-hearted.
For example, *With all due respect . . .* Or *You don't say.*
Or *I'd be glad to hear about it some other time.* They're
not per se sarcastic (though anything can be said in a
sarcastic way) or bristling, like the by-now comical *Excuse ME!* with that *me* woundedly emphasized. What
goes with them, rather, is a slightly too-earnest polite-
ness, a tense wariness, or a telltale flat tone.

They're the ritual insincerities of conversation, not so
much little white lies as little gray hypocrisies, used to
cover up other emotions—or lack of emotion. They're
self-protective or distancing civilities, or perfunctory little sighs of uninterest *(not* disinterest), indicators that

the speaker doesn't quite share the interest, focus, or friendliness of the other person.

What do these standard civilities hide? Anything from anger to wariness, distrust, weariness, distraction, momentary boredom, or total apathy. They could also be deemed little cries for escape if not for good riddance. The person using the expression wishes he or she weren't there, or had already left, or didn't have to deal with who or what prompted the remark. Or they're attempts to avoid, to head off, to minimize "engagement." Rather then being parting (or Parthian) shots, they're more like shots across the bow.

What can we call these common, properly decorous catchphrases that are neither mean nor "edged" but are usually not completely honest or sincere either? Thanks-but-no-thanks-isms? Cover lines?

Whatever we call them, the times when we find ourselves using them (or hearing them) are, well, less-than-happy ones: When we meet somebody we welcome as much as strichnine. When somebody is imposing at an inconvenient time. When we have no interest whatsoever in what somebody's opinion is. When we're being given something we don't want—or not from that person, at least. When we're thoroughly bored or worn out. When we're suspicious or not glad to see that somebody suddenly arrived. When we've been interrupted and want to get back to what we were saying. When we're frustrated and eager to be gone. When a stranger approaches whom we don't trust. When we're responding rotely to somebody going on and on but are not really listening. When we know we're supposed to say something nice. When we want something but have to pretend that we don't want it.

When we want out.

What we really need more of are wittily equivocal lines, the kind that can have two meanings. The great literary critic Edmund Wilson grew weary of being sent manuscripts by people who wanted his praise or patronage. He had reply cards printed up. They thanked the pest for sending whatever the undiscovered masterpiece was and closed with "I shall lose no time in reading it."

But the rest of us seem to be stuck with less imaginative expressions for less-than-happy situations. Here are a number of them. Nary a one is unfamiliar to your ears, and probably not to your lips, either. We all depend on them. But we hardly give them any thought as being our standard dialogue lines of social hypocrisy, wariness, or disenchantment, and they're interesting for that reason. Become more conscious of how frequently you hear some of these—and of what's really going on between people in those situations. To be a watcher of language is to become a student of human beings.

With all due respect . . . When this is said, the respect due may not be much. This introductory phrase is basically a pro forma curtsey to pave the way for criticism or letting somebody really have it. Two other expressions in this category are *Don't take this the wrong way,* which really tells somebody to try not to get too angry; and *I beg to differ,* a slightly stiffer prelude to disagreeing—and who's begging?

I'm sure you are (it is, they will, etc.). Is the sayer really sure? Not hardly. He's, she's, usually humoring the other person or doesn't have much interest in the whole business. This is a weary little pat on the head. Similar to this yawning verbal nod are *You don't say, How nice, How interesting,* and *Is that so?*

Maybe another time. Or preferably never? This is an indispensable escape expression. Hollow as it is, it continues to be used. Also in this category are *I'll be glad to hear about it some other time, I think I'll pass, This is not a good time for me,* and *I'll have to pass, I'm afraid.*

To tell you the truth is a common conversational introductory phrase, but it's usually not introductory to telling the truth. More commonly, it announces a desperate explanation or excuse that's just come to mind.

Feigned praise or congratulations can sometimes be required, and nothing does the job like *I'm just green with envy.* Now, people aren't always insincere, but usu-

ally somebody green with envy is more like gray with
apathy but polite enough to be polite. Other stock gush-
ing phrases are *I'm so happy for you, How wonderful!*
and the passionate *Isn't that nice.*

What do you do when you're offered or presented
with something you don't at all want, whether it's a
favor or a gift, and you have to reject it? You say *Thanks
but no thanks.* No, you can't say that. You say, *But I
appreciate it just the same.*

But sometimes somebody is insistent on giving you
something or doing something for you, somebody you
don't like or don't want any involvement or entangle-
ment with. It's time to say, carefully, *I'd really rather you
didn't bother.* You usually have to follow this up with *No
—really, I'd rather you didn't.* This applies to that repug-
nant cousin who starts to give you a back rub and to the
menacing street entrepreneur suddenly squeegeeing
your windshield in the middle of an intersection. Con-
versely, when you're offered something you'd really like,
it's time to say *I couldn't possibly accept it.* You most
possibly could, but every gift offering seems to entail a
little hypocrisy of one kind or another. After you
couldn't possibly have accepted it but have, it's time to
say *You really shouldn't have.*

May I help you? seems simple and cordial enough, but
often the person tendering it is crying for help, not offering it. When you wander into some place—we won't
say sneak in—where you don't belong, you succeed in
looking innocent for only so long. But the person con-
fronting you doesn't say *What do you think you're doing
here?* or *Have you valid or authorized business on these
premises?* She or he says *May I help you?* Better yet,
Excuse me, please—may I help you? Or *Is there something
I can do for you?* Help is not at all what's in mind.

A little more pointed than this is *Do you have a problem?* In the situations relevant here, this can mean anything from *Is there some reason why you're annoyingly
hanging around here?* to *You look insane to me and I may
soon call the security guard.* As with the expression just

above, more distancing yet is *Excuse me, do you have a problem?* Note: Putting an *excuse me* in front always seems to make a remark, however literally polite, a bit more edged or antagonistic.

Another interesting amenity used as a buffer, sometimes with a shrug, is *Whatever you say.* Have you ever noticed how rarely you ever hear this said with any enthusiasm? It doesn't usually mean so much *I'll do anything you ask* as *I'm just going along for the bumpy ride since this is a situation I can't fight or get out of.* It bespeaks not dedication but resignation.

Being interrupted in conversation is one of the plights of life, and the cry for help here is *As I was saying . . .* or *Getting back to what I was saying . . .* Of course, it's usually only the interruptee who cares about getting back to what was being said. Or *Anyway . . .* It's any way indeed.

What can I say? is one of the most interesting responses we have in English. It is used variously to connote helplessness, bemusement, noninvolvement, self-excusing, regret but not exactly sympathy, or literally having nothing to impart. It's heard from apologetic friends, detached observers, and sharp wheeler-dealers in business. What can I say?

Sometimes you're called upon to do a favor, but it's really to bite the bullet. Somebody imposes on you. What do you say? *Of course you're not imposing.* (When you really don't mind, you're more likely to say, *Come on, I'm happy to help* or *It's my pleasure* or *I don't want to hear another word about it.*) What about *It's no trouble at all*? Is that usually said sincerely or with gritted teeth? Whichever, it's one of these formalities that often is a little deficient in candor.

Now it's time to leave. One of the classic thanks-but-no-thanks lines of American culture is *Don't call us, we'll call you.* But I'll just close with *I'll be in touch.* If you have any arguments or questions, maybe some other time, I think I'll pass, we must have lunch sometime. I'm not at home now, but you can leave a message after the beep.

The deliberately misspelled word in last week's column was *Pavillion* (in *Dorothy Chandler Pavillion*). It's *Pavilion*.

UNCERTAIN ENGLISH

WORD OF THE WEEK: *bumf* or *bumph* (British)—dreary paperwork

QUOTE OF THE WEEK: "In language there is a spice of spelling."

—GEOFFREY GRIGSON

It was a legendary television talk-show host who once said of his nightly performance, "I just keep talking until I have something to say."

The American spirit is indomitable, even when it comes to using the English language.

I come before you this week to talk not only of excessive talk but of uncontrollable conversational hesitation-forms, redundancy, midsentence self-interjections, waffling bailouts, the hysterical present, and above all (in next week's column) of rampantly spreading ask-toning. I come to consider a little-discussed mainstream dialect of English: uncertain English.

Actually, in genuine uncertain English, that last sentence might read thus: "Uh, let's see, I sort of come to, like consider, you know, um, a little-discussed mainstream dialect—okay?—of, like, mainstream English, or something?"

We all speak uncertain English, though it will be a sad day when we begin to write it. Uncertain English is not the broken or defective English of a foreigner, nor is it ungrammatical English. It is the hesitant or meandering English of a native English speaker. It is maundering, which is very different from laundering.

It's in the very nature of oral communication between human beings that much of it be tentative, inexact, finding its way. Spontaneous response, rather than measured reflection, is at work, and there are bound to be false starts and little stumblings in one's wording. The urgencies of thinking on your feet are different from those of writing in your seat, for even with deadlines writing English is a more deliberative, structured mode of expression. To think well on your feet, moreover, isn't necessarily to be articulate on your feet. To be quick or voluble is not necessarily to be clear and compact. That uncertain English can always creep in.

And nowadays it seems to be leaping in, not creeping in. There are certain earmarks—or is it lipmarks?—to insecure speech, and I 'ear them everywhere in Woofton. Various symptoms and in particular two new ones —the addiction to *like* and the phenomenon of ask-toning—suggest that more people are more insecure about their communicating than they've ever been.

The most obvious symptoms of hesitation or uncertainty in speech are those throat-clearing vocables (or subarticulations) we all let slip; *um, mmm, uh,* and *well,* chiefly, but sometimes *so* as well. (Literature, curiously, seems to prefer *er,* but how many of us say the literary *er*?) These sentence-starters or -fillers are called hesitation-forms, and they're nothing new or recent. In severe cases, those uncultivated *um*s, *mmm*s, *uh*s, and *well*s become cultivated mannerisms, a kind of intentional stutter for effect. For what effect, is the question. The British upper-class stammer (or traulism) is a legendary mannerism. We Americans prefer classless hemming and hawing. The speech of one of New York City's recent mayors was always laced with um-and-ums.

Gestures, facial expressions, and general body language can also be relied on to compensate for uncertainty in verbal communicating. People who are a little

intraverted about getting their message across in words
—or always feel a need to emphasize it—often do a lot
of flailing and face acting. Intonation, also, is something
we all depend on to make sure there's no uncertainty
about our message. It's all part of nonverbal communication, a field known as paralanguage or paralinguistics.

Silence, or long pauses, would seem to be the likely
result when there is uncertainty about what one is trying
to say. But it's not. The eloquent pause is the exception
rather than the rule. Most people do one of two things:
They become repetitiously wordy, or they interject
needless phrases that ask for reassurance from the listener.

Redundancy is the term for repetitious wordiness, and
redundancy is often a symptom of uncertainty. Reitera-
tion can be valid for emphasis, but sometimes it is point-
less, and it is not hard to find in writing as well as in
spoken English. When you are told that Mr. Joe Blow
was hospitalized for half a year and then again that he
was a patient for six months, you've run into redundancy, otherwise known as tautology. The more a
person repeats or rephrases, the more that person's con-
viction and confidence, and possibly even credibility,
may be called into question. (Pathological repetitious-
ness, where mental illness is involved, is called palilalia
or verbigeration.)

Another motif of maundering can be pleonasm.
Whereas tautology is repeating a thought in different
words, pleonasm is merely adding on needless words, as
by saying *combine together* instead of *combine,* which
needs no further togetherness; or *resultant effect* instead
of *effect.* English is full of pleonastic expressions, among
them *past history, past experience, free gift, future plans,
revert back, consensus of opinion, old adage, add in, can-
cel out, hollow tube, far distance,* and *personal friend.*
When you think about it, even *mental telepathy* and *the
reason why* are pleonasms. But people don't do a lot of
thinking about it, particularly in the drift of conversation. Such redundant expressions are so common and

reflexive with many people that they don't necessarily reflect uncertainty. But maybe a grain of uncertainty?

At least initially, a lack of confidence in one's English —or in one word being sufficient to do the job—may also account for the prevalence of such ingrained pleonasms as *hue and cry, beck and call, vim and vigor.* These are redundant pairs joined by an *and.* The two words in question may not be precise synonyms—in the case of *bag and baggage,* for instance, the former originally referred to personal belongings and the latter to military ones, a distinction few are aware of today. But they are virtual synonyms and hence offer tried and true (there's another) expressions that are basically punchy redundancies with a little alliterative or rhyming jingle to them. Others we use—for a little uncertain emphasis?— are *candor and frankness, aid and abet, various and sundry, in this day and age, if and when, dribs and drabs, over and above, one and the same, fair and square, plain and obvious, trim and tidy, fine and dandy, first and foremost, sum and substance, cruel and inhuman, kith and kin, part and parcel, might and main, in any shape or form, of any sort or kind, each and every, for all intents and purposes, dead and gone, alas and alack, fear and trembling, ways and means, frills and furbelows, leaps and bounds, heart and soul,* and *calm, cool, and collected.* (H. W. Fowler calls these "Siamese twins.") You know, we use them twixt and tween, the whole kit and kaboodle, and so forth and so on? (A pairing of contrasting terms, by the way, such as *now and then, black and white, the ins and outs,* or *here and there,* is called a merism.)

This tendency to pair up virtual mean-alikes is the bread and butter of traditional legal prose. A lawyer will never write, "If any person intentionally harms the owner . . ." when he or she can write, "If any person, individual, or party intentionally, purposely, deliberately, intentfully, or premeditatedly harms, hurts, injures, or does damage to the owner, possessor . . ." (A wonderful old word for such battering legalese is *grimgribber.*) In law, of course, this numbing synonymomania is a way of covering all the bases, or covering one's asterisk. Or is it a way of covering uncertainty, which in this literal case could be serious or expensive uncertainty?

But a more palpable trait of uncertain English is the self-interjection—the interrupting or trailing of one's own statement with a questioning tag in order to be sure of the listener's attention or comprehension: *But a more, you know, palpable trait of uncertain English is, okay, the self-interjection—you know what I mean?* These are little, slightly insecure attention-checks. (They check listener loyalty, and they check, or stop up, the flow of thought.) They include *you know, okay, right, you see,* and *you know what I mean.* Present-day American speech, far more than British speech I'd say, is full of them.

Postpositive (or after-placed) expressions such as . . . *don't you?,* . . . *won't you?,* and . . . *doesn't she?* are normal and appropriate English. They're called tag questions or question tags. But self-interjected tags are hiccups of verbal insecurity. They're a bad habit, and the more unconscious they are—if never to the irritated listener—the worse the prognosis. *Okay* is the latest and most trendy usage here. From being a proudful Americanism signaling approval or positive energy, it has been adapted domestically as an interruptive tic of insecurity, or one to be tacked on after every ten words or so, okay? But the most epical of attention-checks is *You understand what I'm saying?* or sometimes *You understand what I'm telling you?* It's long and unwieldy, but there seem to be many Americans who feel the need to say it after every other sentence, like a nervous thumb and forefinger grabbing at somebody's lapel.

Another characteristic of uncertain American English is what I call the waffling bailout. Waffling bailouts are those little afterthought phrases that people tack on when they know or fear they're being imprecise or incorrect: *or something, or anything, or like that, and all, and everything.* These are really uneasy subjoiners, af-

ternonthoughts (not at all the same as afternoon
thoughts). Sometimes they're like lazy *et ceteras*. If they
haven't become an individual's unconscious speech
mannerism, they get tagged onto a sentence out of some
sense of possible vagueness—and succeed in making the
sentence yet more vague: *He's a scientist or something.
They like going out to restaurants and all.* As mental drib-
bles at the ends of questions, *or what* and *or anything* are
popular: *Will they be returning to the country club or
what?* And there are those two bailouts used before
rather than after, *sort of* and *kind of,* as in *She's kind of
an artist.* Well, we don't want to be offensively precise,
do we?

The latest entrant here is *or whatever,* but you don't
need to be told that. Millions of people today feel that
no matter how heartfelt or important what they've just
said is, it's only an *either.* It requires the addition of a
vague *or.* The question is, Is *or whatever* being overused
because of mere uncertainty or insecurity, or out of
sheer mental and verbal laziness? Whichever (not whatever), or-whateverism has spread like wildfire or whatever. Some observers predict that by the year 2000, *or
whatever* may be the first two words that most American
newborns learn to say. Whatever a way to start life!

Only mention will be made here of the new all-purpose slough-off word being dropped every which way
into spoken English, *like.* Any kind of pause or silence
seems to be embarrassing to many people, and *like* is
being used, with a dull dispassion, to stave it off. Several
interpretations of its by-now reflexive overuse are possible. But there is no question that in many instances *like*
is interjected repeatedly as a kind of prefix signaling
uncertainty—regarding either oneself or the person one
is talking to. (*Like* was the subject of a previous
Wordwizard column.)

Another characteristic of uncertain English is the tendency to rely on the present tense in relating news or
experiences. Instead of *I was on my way to work when
this woman raced across the crosswalk . . . ,* one says,

I'm on my way to work, okay, when this woman races across the crosswalk, okay . . . People have always done this in conversation, of course, particularly less educated people. But more people than ever present-tense everything nowadays, as if they're uneasy beyond the immediate here-and-now. They regard the past tense as the tense past. It could be just a habit, but I think a certain uncertainty is at work here. It's not the so-called historical present. It's the hysterical present.

Which brings us to the newest symptom of uncertain English. It's tonal rather than verbal. It's a rising inflection of rising inflections. It's—for want of a better term—ask-toning?

The question mark tells all. See next week's column.

The deliberately misspelled word in last week's column was *strichnine*. It's *strychnine*.

ASK-TONING

WORD OF THE WEEK: *ben trovato*—a charming or memorable but untrue anecdote

QUOTE OF THE WEEK: "Learn to write well, or do not write at all."

—JOHN SHEFFIELD

A whole column not about words but about mere intonation?

Yes, because it concerns one of the great linguistic mysteries of our time.

Last time out I ventured some observations regarding uncertain English and its symptoms, including tautology and pleonasms, hesitation-forms such as *uh,* self-interjections such as *you know,* waffling bailouts such as *or something* (and spreading or-whateverism), and the hysterical present. This left the most recent and interesting aspect of insecure speech. I call it ask-toning?

That last sentence should end with a period?

Not if it's being uttered by America's younger generation in the new, questioning or ask-toning tone of voice.

You may have noticed how many people under, say, thirty today have a curious habit of making the most ordinary statement sound, up and up at the close of the sentence, like a question? Not *I was over at the library today* (period), but *I was over at the library today?* (question mark).

If you haven't noticed that nationally there is a rising infliction of rising inflection, it's perhaps because you yourself are young and ask-tone your speech all the time without noticing? So that you don't even notice that in day-to-day conversation a lot of harmless declarative utterances are pitched, in both senses of that word, like interrogative ones?

It's an interesting phenomenon? Or possibly it's a questionable one? It continues to be a bit of a mystery to language-watchers, and this column does not pretend to have all the answers? Or rather, it doesn't pretend to have all the questions?

No more unexpected question marks here to make the point. Ask-toning may be scarily natural in conversation to baby-grandboomers, but in writing—I'm already exhausted and asked-out. Maybe, after the above ask-toned paragraph, you are too. (But if you read on here, you'll be rewarded with my solution to the mysterious cause of epidemic ask-toning.)

Negativity is a very popular word nowadays, but maybe there should be some talk about interrogativity. Have the speechways of a whole nation ever been so overwhelmingly affected by a rising inflection? Evidence of youthful ask-toning doubtless can be found earlier, but its rapid spread across the United States unquestionably (and questioningly) occurred in the decade of the 1980s. From which direction? There are strong suspicions that it first took hold in California. California is always the prime suspect for American language quakes, from beat generation lingo to flower children talk to 1970s (Marin County) psychobabble to surfer and Valley Girl talk. Could ask-toning be an outgrowth of that girlishing vowel-flattening Valley Girl glug-glug?

The second question here, besides the one of origin or origins, is the analytic or interpretive one. What is really going on when an otherwise normal individual voices most of his or her simple informational statements, personal comments, and conversational responses as if they were questions?

Does ask-toning reflect factual and educational insecurity? Underlying (psychological) self-doubt and a
need for constant reassurance? Wariness and suspicion?
A kind of sentence-by-sentence solicitousness toward
one's listener? A defensively quizzical pose? A curiously
new way to appear to be cool and uncommitted? Or is it
just a new speech habit that's proved to be remarkably
contagious and has no particular deep meaning or moti-
vation behind it?

All of the above?

The possible explanations are certainly interesting.
This is no conventional little language mystery. It's not
merely a question as to where a particular pronunciation originated or who first used a particular trendy
word. It's a mystery that has to do with an intonational
change—upturn?—in the way millions of Americans utter complete thoughts, a latter lilt that appears to have
asked its way into U.S. speech habits over the course of
a mere decade.

Behind ask-toning, moreover, lie questions having
definite psychological and philosophical dimensions. Is
it posturing? Or is it a cry for help from an uneasy generation?

Not too long ago on the op-ed page of *The New York
Times*, novelist Lynne Sharon Schwartz offered her
speculations about ask-toning. After touching on "inflection inflation" as a sign that students today are no
longer sure of anything and need constant reassurance
that what they're saying is worthy of attention, she
raised other interesting possibilities. One was that it
showed a failure of "fortitude or endurance to argue a
point or sustain a narrative." Another was that it
showed, among ask-toners, a distrust of the spoken
word—of good old plain English. Whichever, Schwartz
leaned toward a sobering conclusion: The rising inflection signals an abdication of responsibility for what one
is saying and could be a disturbing trend. What if, in
speech or in writing, our government officials took to
ask-toning their reports, statements, answers?

Journalism professor James Gorman also has had his say in a *New York Times* piece on what he termed *up-talk* (although *up-talk* could easily be misunderstood as a term for brightly optimistic or euphemistic language). Pointing out that rising inflections have a history among the Irish, English, and southern American upper middle-class, he noted yet other explanations being advanced.

Ask-toning, Gorman says, might fundamentally be a vocal styling keyed to the listener, either a kind of deference or "inclusiveness" or a way of establishing that the listener is interested or on the same wave length. Or it could be, egoistically, a signal that more is coming—don't interrupt. Then again, Gorman says, some people think it's mostly an attempt to be "cool, ironic, uncommitted." On the other hand, Deborah Tannen, a best-selling author of books on communication between the sexes, thinks it may be a mistake to read too much into the rising inflection: It has most likely spread just because it's oddly contagious and people tend to be imitative in their speech habits.

How many other language issues of these or any times have as many as a baker's dozen possible explanations?

Reviewing the options, do you think ask-toning has become so prevalent because younger Americans: (1) are feeling insecure about their facts, information, or education; (2) need reassurance that what they're saying is worthy of attention; (3) are cynically defensive and thus wary or suspicious of the listener; (4) are trying to affect being cool, detached, skeptical, or uncommitted; (5) lack the confidence or intellectual stamina to sustain an argument or narrative or even a couple of declarative sentences; (6) have no trust in words or conventional communication; (7) don't want to be held responsible for anything they say; (8) are being solicitous toward the listener, to make sure they're being understood from sentence to sentence; (9) need to feel sure that the listener is "coming from" the same place and is hence an ally worthy of the effort of talking; (10) just want to signal they have more to say and don't want to be interrupted; (11) are afraid that using normal declarative inflections will seem "offensively" pushy or elitist; (12) have just picked it up as a habit, there being absolutely no motive or psychological reason behind it except peer pressure; or (13) want to sound "questioning" to appear young, innocent, and nice?

The greater question is whether only one of these explanations could be the single correct one, rather than several or even all of them.

Meanwhile, it's worth considering some recent changes in American society that may have some bearing on a new attraction to speaking with a rising, questioning, or self-questioning inflection.

The U.S. population has been evolving into a more multiethnic one, and confident spoken English may be becoming more the exception than the norm. Apart from our transformation into a less homogeneous society, much has been written and said about a general decline in educational standards and performance nationally, even in rudimentary language and mathematical skills. If Americans used to talk about maximal self-confidence, they now seem to talk more about minimal self-esteem (and role models). Media have become a main medium of life "experience" (or vicarious experience), and for younger people longer television-watching hours—and channel-surfing—seem to have created ever-shorter attention spans. Infotainment and theme parks are everywhere and are not the same as real information or education. There is a lot of expertise in superficial, present-time-locked pop culture and less in genuine culture.

These and other factors could well account for the new inflectional uncertainty. Or is it a question not of uncertainty but of cynicism, an irresoluteness about the troubled world today? Is ask-toning a symptom of *ressentiment?*

Resent a what?

Ressentiment, a French borrowing found in the un-abridged *Random House Dictionary,* is defined thus: "1. any cautious, defeatist, or cynical attitude based on the belief that the individual and human institutions exist in a hostile or indifferent universe or society. 2. an oppressive awareness of the futility of trying to improve one's status in life or in society."

Of course, there are at least two other possible theories to be mentioned apropos of ask-toning. One is that the rise in voice reflects a strange desire in young people to be living in prepuberty again. The other is that ask-toning is actually a new style, or timbre, of your basic whining.

But you've been patient in fielding all these speculations about one of the great mysteries of contemporary American civilization and deserve to know the real cause of ask-toning: a late-supper-hour television show on which millions of speech-vulnerable young Americans have grown up.

Jeopardy! is that successful game show noteworthy for being careful to avoid calling itself a quiz show or have any buzzing sounds, for having a name (and the horse-racing term *daily double*) that has nothing in particular to do with the nature of the show—and for having the gimmick of contestants' phrasing their answers in the form of questions. It's "America's favorite answer-and-question show."

Clearly, this answering-by-questioning formula has had too great an effect on younger Americans.

Seeing, every weekday evening, three bright people flaunt their encyclopedic (if superficial) knowledge but, perversely, always in the form of questions has warped normal conversational inflections. Intonationally, it has brainwashed millions of people into a backward habit: thinking of answers as being questions. It has created the malaise of ask-toning.

It's all Alex Trebek's fault.

The deliberately misspelled word in last week's column was *intraverted.* It's *introverted.*